GLIMPSING
INTO THE
KINGDOM

A Series on Kingdom Parables

PAUL HARRINGTON

WESTBOW
PRESS
A DIVISION OF THOMAS NELSON

WestBow Press books may be ordered through booksellers or by contacting:

WestBow Press
A Division of Thomas Nelson
1663 Liberty Drive
Bloomington, IN 47403
www.westbowpress.com
1 (866) 928-1240

ISBN: 978-1-4908-1060-7 (sc)
ISBN: 978-1-4908-1061-4 (hc)
ISBN: 978-1-4908-1059-1 (e)

Library of Congress Control Number: 2013918358

Printed in the United States of America.

WestBow Press rev. date: 10/17/2013

TABLE OF CONTENTS

PROLOGUE

The idea for this writing came from a series I taught at Brookridge Community Church, in Haverhill, MA, at the urging of Dr. Steve Squires, the pastor of the church. Four teachings came from that series. Two more came at the request of Dr. Rustin Comer, who, at his church in California, wanted to offer a sermon series on Kingdom parables through the six-week season of Lent in 2010. Finally, another came to mind while on vacation.

Having taught these lessons as sermons, it was then the task to get them to make sense as written lessons. It is my desire that these lessons be useful to pastors and teachers in either of two ways, one as a sermon series (though each can be adapted and used independently of the others), the other as group lessons.

There are seven parables investigated in this study. My aim here is not to give the definitive interpretation of Jesus' teachings on the kingdom of God (or heaven), but to come to an understanding of something I believe is most overlooked in these stories. We have a role in the kingdom of God, in the here and now, and we have a dynamic purpose in bringing about its fulfillment. God is inviting us into His story right now. For too long, too many of us have thought of the kingdom of

God in terms of concrete visuals—streets paved with gold, pearls at every gate—or as a spiritual, eternal reward at the end of a long, narrow, difficult road. The teachings Jesus left to us bear none of that. Jesus tended to focus His attention on the activity of the kingdom. As a result, it is necessary for us to understand who we are in that kingdom that God has created and is creating. We are very good at inviting people to the kingdom, but very poor at communicating just what that kingdom is.

Kingdom parables are best taken as imagery. Indeed, as Jesus taught these concepts, he drew on multiple sources to convey his ideas: poetry, visual aids, and story-telling, among others. As I have prepared these lessons, I have attempted to do the same. I have used buckets of soil, photos of plants, live interviews, poetry recitation, and other devices to get across the ideas. It is my desire that as others use the material, leaders would be as creative as possible. I believe it is much easier to connect with these teachings if we approach them less as literal concepts and more as figurative truths. As we share these thoughts, it is essential that we let the mystery of them speak to the listeners.

A common trait of the kingdom parables is that they avoid any semblance of conveying discipline, obedience and legality. The phrase "kingdom of God" never leads to behavioral benchmarks. Jesus does not use these teachings to say, "In the kingdom of God, people will do this, but they can't do that." He does not say with them, "If you are a kingdom citizen, you can say this, but you cannot say that." Instead, He consistently uses the kingdom stories to create a vision of who we can be and what we are called to be about. This is a difficulty for those of us who want to know what the rules are in this new life. I believe that to truly understand the kingdom parables we have to recognize that they are about vision— God's vision and how we fit into that.

The first chapter is not about any kingdom parable, but about my experience of the kingdom. For us to lead a full and rich discussion of the kingdom, I believe we need to understand our own personal legacies, our own successes and failures as people of God, our own adventure with the King of kings. In sharing my story, I hope that it will lead others to earnestly connect their own stories in the kingdom. From that place of honesty, the rest becomes more meaningful.

In the parable chapters, I have included section headings for use on a screen. They are in boldface. I tend to put only general thoughts or phrases on the screen as I teach more in depth. For the sake of suggestion, these can be found as separate lines or indents, offset from the paragraphs surrounding them. Oftentimes, I use photos underneath the verbiage because pictures can convey supportive ideas very quickly. Also, I have kept all the lessons a particular length so that they can be presented in 45 minutes or less. For the purposes of group study, I have included questions at the end of each chapter. I can honestly say that the questions came to me as I reread the lessons, asking myself, "What would I like to explore further if I had the chance, or if I were sitting around with a group of friends?" These questions are suggestions, as well, for ways in which the lessons might be modified to fit the needs of groups who, perhaps, may need to explore particular spiritual issues in a different light.

Finally, I added some thoughts in order to try to make some sense of the collection of teachings. I believe Jesus had in mind that this new kingdom of God would be like none before and that the disciples, of all people, really needed to catch the vision, well, sometime before the Ascension. Without giving anything away, these teachings were squarely aimed at moving us beyond a narcissistic view of covenant with God. (For instance, when God said, "I will be your God, you will be my people,"—see Ex. 6:7 and Jer. 7:23—each of us tends to hear 'you' and 'your' as singular, and 'people' really means 'person,' as in 'me.' That is a vanity we cannot afford as kingdom people.) This last section, then, looks at the impact of these teachings on us as individuals *within the larger kingdom.*

It is my sincere desire to strengthen the kingdom community as groups explore Jesus' teachings together. Some of His teachings are rather cryptic, and where two people of faith disagree on interpretation, there is opportunity to share together in the learning process. As I mentioned, these are not in any way definitive, but I do hope they encourage dialog. Even more I hope they inspire within us the desire to say, "Yes, I want to be part of that. That is a King I'd give my life for."

ACKNOWLEDGMENTS

This book would not have come to completion without the aid and encouragement of many people. Foremost, I want to thank Dr. Steve Squires for opening his pulpit to me and giving me the topic of study to pursue. Dr. Rustin Comer inspired me to look into more of the parables, to look closely at the body of them as a whole. It was my friend John Carlson who suggested that this be converted from a series of spoken teachings into a book. After that, there were countless friends and family who read, edited, questioned, and challenged. Among them, I am most grateful to Andrew Drenas and Jim Warren, who both read my manuscript on more than one occasion and made critical comments on content, grammar and style. I am thankful to my family for all their encouragement. My wife Angie, sister Rachael, sons Sean and Brad, and my mother Barbara all read the chapters as I printed them and urged me to keep going. My mother-in-law Anne, gave me confidence precisely when I needed it. Finally, I must thank Mary Wegener, at Westbow Press, who has been more than attentive to this process, gave me space when I needed it, and a nudge when I needed that. Thank you all.

—Paul Harrington

CHAPTER 1

Experiencing Kingdom

I cannot say for sure the day I accepted Jesus as Lord. I *could* say it was the day I went forward in church to get baptized. But that would be a half-truth at best. I went forward because my next older brother went up the week before; typical for me, I could not stand him having the attention, so I just had to go up. I *could* say it was the night I went forward after a particularly rousing revival sermon, to rededicate my life after a few years of mere dabbling in religion. But that would be a misdirection. I had no intention of doing anything different; I just knew I shouldn't keep on the same course. And I *could* say it was the moment in therapy, ten years after that, that I experienced the overwhelming grace of knowing I don't measure up, won't measure up, can't measure up and because of His Love,

I don't have to.

But that would be incomplete, because that moment would not have come if all the moments before it had not led me to that time and place.

The reality for me is that my journey in Christ has been one of progressive revelation. My earliest observation of Jesus, God, redemption, community and the whole faith "thing" was viewed through the lens of a sin-sick or world-weary worldview. We all have that lens. We all come to Christ, *when* we come to Christ, from a distorted, twisted place—clearly some more twisted than others. That's the lens through which we get our view of the world. The lens not only distorts our observation of the world, it distorts our experience of it. Even more, it distorts our approach to the scripture. So the two main ways God speaks to us, our experience of creation and our experience of His written word, are distorted from the truth by the lenses we insist on using. For me, getting to a healthy view of God's love in Christ has taken, and is taking, a lot of work to remove that lens.

My Salvation

One of the eye-opening truths I have had to come to terms with, in the process of removing that lens, is that my salvation really is not about me. My statement of faith (Jesus is Lord), my journey, my faith, my ministry—all of these terms are important, yet they are just shadows of the Truly Significant. What is relevant about me in the larger scheme of "all things Christ" is *how I fit into* all things Christ. When I trivialize my salvation experience to be what Jesus has done for *me*, I move the focus from Jesus to me. I have decided that is not how I am to be a Christ follower.

When we first come rushing headlong into the arms of Jesus, it is only natural to feel the rush of elation, "the joy of salvation" we call it, and long to tell our friends about what Jesus has done for us. To know that the holy Son of God, the one who alone is both fully God and completely human, knows us better than we know ourselves to the very core of our beings and loves us anyway, that is truly something to shout about.

But something happens along the way. That yearning to share our slice of good news with those closest to us—our community—gets subdued by our desire to do things right. At some spiritual place along the way, our passion to make sure that other people know is pushed to the background, and to the foreground comes the need to make sure we are getting ourselves right with God. We turn from being other-centered to self-centered.

In claiming salvation for myself, I have claimed salvation *for myself.* Is that really what Jesus wanted of me?

It's Not About *Me*?

I still struggle with this. I suspect I am not the only one. (I know you all thought it was about me too. Sure you did.) In a very real way, I am convinced God knows me intimately. I know this from my experience of Him in times of great spiritual awareness. And I know this from the promises laid out for us in scripture. I love this about God—how with all the things going on both profound and miniscule, He would care enough to notice one so small as me. "Oh, what is Man that You are mindful of him?" (Ps 8:4)

It is very tempting to take that next step and make my spiritual journey about me, but wisdom says no. To make my faith about me, and my needs, and my hurts, and my goals, would be perhaps like replacing that world-weary lens with a mirror. A foggy mirror at that. I know there are things about me God would like to transform, and seems to exert a lot of energy to do so, given my stubbornness, but it is too much to think that the transformation is purely for my benefit.

There really is a much larger picture here. It is an image of a passionately loving God, yearning for His children. The beautiful thing about God's story is that it is plural. There is "We-ness" to it—God and His children.

Where Do I Fit?

In all the sayings of Jesus and the writings about him, there is very little language, if any, that conveys to us the thought, "just you and me, God." Even when Jesus entertained conversations with individuals, such as Nicodemus (John 3) or the woman at the well (John 4), He spoke in more global language. When Nicodemus asked, "Jesus, what must I do to . . . ?" not once was Jesus recorded as saying, "You must have a personal relationship with me." Rebirth is not a solo act. In being born again, we experience the kingdom of God. Kingdoms are not made of a king and one subject; kingdoms imply multitudes. In the conclusion to His conversation with the woman He met at a well, Jesus spoke of worshipers—those whom God seeks—who worship in spirit and in truth. In these two conversations, and in many others, Jesus took individuals into the realm of faith and showed them the larger God-community.

I believe that is how I fit in. My salvation is about me only in that it was my experience to bring me into the realm of a much broader community. A movement. Beyond that, my salvation is not my own. Not really. It is God's salvation of creation, and He has invited me into it. I can hardly believe it, and I am excited by the thought of it. Even better, I am thrilled by the experience of it (when I allow myself the privilege). And it is made all the more excellent in that I do not experience this alone. *We share in this together!*

It Is About *Us*

It is an often-overlooked truth that Jesus came to redeem the world. When He taught, He almost always used the word 'you' in the plural form. We give lip-service to that nugget of information, but then we proceed right on with the solo-journey mostly without regard to the larger community of faith. The consequences are evident: a small minority of believers is empowered to do the large majority of the work; a large number of believers feel their faith experience is private, not to be shared; a great many believers feel no responsibility to the community around them. We could go on.

It is no wonder that the majority of Jesus' teachings are centered on the kingdom of God. When even faith becomes an area of self-indulgence, teaching needs to address the shocking truth: faith is not about you or me. It is about God, and God loves *us*. In His kingdom teachings, Jesus uses astounding images to expose profound truths about the reign and realm of God. The most powerful point of all, fundamental to the rest, is that in God's kingdom

God

    Wants

        Us

           With

                Him.

We need to own that. It is exciting!

Communicating the Kingdom

Jesus spent a good portion of His teaching inviting us to take part in the kingdom. What exactly did He mean? When we share our stories of faith with others, what do we hope will be the result? Those two questions may be one. We need to understand what Jesus has invited us into, and we need to be clear what we are inviting others into.

Truly, the kingdom teachings declare the wonder of heaven and proclaim the marvel that is God. There is beauty there, there is joy, there is sorrow and grief to overcome, all conveyed in His teaching. At the same time, there is the wondrous truth that those who do not deserve even the merest consideration are brought into the presence of the King.

At the heart of it all is a gracious God who longs to lavish his love on all those who would welcome him. He yearns for us, seeks us, and prepares a place for us in His most intimate space.

Truly this is a kingdom to end all kingdoms, and a King worthy of our most honest worship.

What is your experience in the kingdom?

CHAPTER 2

The Kingdom Family

What Kind of Family *Is* This?

In the synoptic gospels we know as Matthew, Mark and Luke, the authors set the kingdom parables in relation to a pivotal moment in the ministry of Jesus, when Jesus steps away from His family of origin. In Mark's gospel, His interaction with family comes just prior to the kingdom teachings of chapter four. We see the same connection in Matthew. The family event here leads into seven kingdom parables and is followed up by another story of Jesus and His family. In Luke, the kingdom stories come before the family event, suggesting that for Luke, the family event was the focal point of the teachings, rather than the event giving meaning to the teachings. The juxtaposition of the stories, though, leads to the inescapable conclusion that the gospel writers saw a connection between this significant "family event" in the life of Jesus, and His concept of the kingdom. It is a connection that is meaningful, and valuable to explore if we truly want to understand the kingdom teachings of Jesus.

Mark 3:31-35

Then His mother and His brothers arrived, and standing outside they sent word to Him and called Him. A crowd was sitting around Him, and they said to Him, "Behold, Your mother and Your brothers are outside looking for You." Answering them, He said, "Who are My mother and My brothers?" Looking about at those who were sitting around Him, He said, "Behold My mother and My brothers! "For whoever does the will of God, he is My brother and sister and mother." (NASB)

As in all of the teachings of Jesus, there are layers here. There is a text and a subtext. The result is that we can look at this text from a number of angles, and get rich meaning. One angle we can take is to look at the event to get guidance on family issues. There is clarity for family systems, family dynamics, family dysfunction, and co dependence, but it does not end there. Though on the surface it seems to be a teaching about family, it carries a profound lesson about the kingdom of God.

Family or Kingdom: What's the Difference?

This is why. For those who heard Jesus that day, and the hearers and readers who followed them, Jesus spoke to them not only about His family, but also about *their* history. The Jewish heritage came to them as both family and nation. God made His covenant, which is the core of the faith, with Abraham. God brought forth, through Abraham, a family, and a nation. For those who heard Jesus that day, family and kingdom were one and the same.

Jesus asked a question that most certainly rocked them: "Who are My mother and My brothers?" Who is My family? The implication, of course, was that His blood relations were not. Was He honestly suggesting that family is not based on blood? Then what is He saying about the kingdom? The gospel accounts give us the impression that Jesus disturbed His audience that day. The Gospel of Matthew is abrupt about it: after the kingdom teachings, he points out the response of the locals—"isn't that Mary's boy?" They might also have been asking, "wasn't his father Joseph, the carpenter?" It is as if they were asking, "Who does he think he is?"

The locals thought of Jesus as merely the son of Mary, with siblings and a little carpentry shop around the corner. Perhaps some of His childhood friends and neighbors thought how Mary must be proud, but they were missing the commanding essence of Jesus. By adopting a condescending posture, they could not recognize the authority of Jesus. And without that authority, the teachings of Jesus would have no impact. In fact, one might hear Him and think He was crazy. His blood relations certainly did by this point.

Even now, if we believe that Jesus was merely Mary's son, or that he was a wise man and a good teacher, then we minimize the person and impact of Jesus. We miss who Jesus is. Jesus brings so much more than fine words. Jesus brings authority to the kingdom of God.

With that authority, Jesus redefines who we are as the people of God. We are no longer people separated by personal agendas, rather we are united as the family of God, as the kingdom of God.

Family and kingdom, one and the same—a chosen race, a royal priesthood, a holy nation, a people for God's own possession (1 Pet 2:9, NIV), *but not because of our bloodlines*. This is a tough concept for us to get. Exactly how does that work?

The Family Ethos

When we enter this scene in Mark 3, we have to ask, what is Jesus troubled about here? What does His family represent that troubles Him? It is, after all, a good Jewish family.

Like all families, there is something that permeates all that the family is about, an ethos, a set of guiding principles. Whether the rules are written out, or go unspoken, they still drive the activity of the family. These rules define the family gods. At the same time, the "family gods"—those things which are revered above all other things and held as unalterable—make the rules. For instance, if booze is the family god, then the rules revolve around protecting the drinkers and the lifestyle of drinking. Conversely, the very rules we live by create a vacuum into which we place the things we value most, our 'gods.' It is inevitable that when we live a drinker's lifestyle, we cannot wait to get to that next experience of drinking.

Each and every family has an ethos defined by spoken and, especially, unspoken rules. Sadly, in most families I know, the rules revolve around addictions and -isms (racism, fascism, pluralism, socialism, hedonism, rationalism—you get the idea), and the roles they create. Or the rules could revolve around money. Or fear. Or shame. Or worry. Or fun. Fun, I think, is the new god that drives the family. If it's not fun, it's not worth doing. Fun has replaced meaning and purpose and joy.

The family gods may also be the heroes that are venerated. And because they are highly thought of, we should all be like them. Never mind that we may not be like the family heroes and that our gifts lay elsewhere. In this system, all that matters is the question, "Why can't I be more like him or her?" In hero worship, the rules revolve around venerating the hero, at the same time creating rules that would protect the hero (for instance, one cannot question the wisdom of the hero or the cost of his or her heroic actions) and require others in the system to mimic the hero. This is deadly to those who do not fit the heroes mold.

Families create roles based on rules and family gods. It is very difficult to break out of those roles. The more toxic the family environment, the tougher it is to break free.

Clinging to the Law

In the Jewish family of Palestine, the ethos was the Law. If you're going to have a family god, that is not a bad one. But it's not a good one either. Through the years, as the Jews were fragmented, the Law became the defining aspect of their lives. It is a very typical thing to do: when life gets crazy, we draw in the boundaries, reset our limits, minimize the potential hurt or damage. For the Jews, the Law was a great thing to cling to. Honor the Law, uphold the Law, *protect* the Law. Clearly, they were in survival mode. They had already been dispersed throughout the Middle East multiple times in their recent past, and now they were under Roman occupation. The Law was the heart of their kingdom.

Jesus taught the Law was not intended to be an end, a way to survive; it was intended to be a beginning, a way of blessing. To Abraham God said, "I will make you a great nation, and your descendants will be a blessing to all the nations." (See Genesis 12: 1-3)

I bless, so that you bless.

Yet for so many people, the Law became the reference point, replacing the Lawgiver.

Clinging to the Past

This is the rub for this passage in Mark: when the family showed up to take Jesus home, they came out of a sense of embarrassment. They were afraid Jesus had gone over the line, and the language suggests perhaps over the deep end. His ideas didn't fit into their framework of faith and family.

While clinging to the Law, the family rules, the family roles, and the family gods, Mary and her children could not let go of the past. Families have a way of doing that. It is the experience of one who goes home for the first time, after having been away for a few years. Typically, he falls back into the same old roles and positions, no matter how hard he may have worked to grow beyond those limitations of the past.

Kingdoms have a way of clinging to the past, too. The ideals that establish a dynasty are most often the ideals that bring it down upon itself, when those ideals are held rigidly in place. Perhaps this is why Thomas Jefferson recommended a revolution every twenty years: he may have foreseen a time when the young republic would need to rethink it's vision so as not to hold too rigidly to the letter of the Constitution.

The hard truth here is that while we would like to use Jesus to justify our rigid, preconceived notions of faith and family, we have to listen very carefully to what He says. "Whoever does the will of God, whoever hears the word (*logos*) of God and does it, *they* are my family." It is not Jesus who must bend to the will of the family; it is the family which is reshaped, ethos and all, gods and all.

It is all too easy to cling to "what has always been." Hunkered down under the umbrella of the family system (however that is shaped), we may never notice the sun is shining. What family dynamics keep us hunkered down, keep us from "[soaring] on wings as eagles?" (Is. 40:31, NIV) Secrecy, shame, a checkered past, unhealthy family gods—these things keep us stuck in the past. Christ wants us to move beyond the past. "Come to me, all who are weary and heavy-laden, and I will give you rest." (Matthew 11:28, NASB)

What Defines You?

Jesus points the family toward moving forward—it is to take action, to serve, to hear the word of God and to do it, to be a blessing to all the nations. His family of origin wanted to define Him by His past; He defines His family by what is to come. Pointing to those who eagerly sit at His feet, He proclaims, "these are my mother and my brothers." He is pointing to the folks who are willing to take the journey with Him.

When you think about who is family to you, is your family dominated by the past or focused on the future? Perhaps it is a mix. I suspect that most families are a mix. But as a family system gets more dysfunctional, the family members are increasingly controlled by the past. Toxic family systems are dominated by toxic rules rooted in the past. At that moment when Jesus asked the question, "Who is my family?" He stepped out of His family system. In that action, He showed us a new way: His purpose was not to destroy His family but to redeem it. Jesus did not come to abolish the Law, but to fulfill it. (Mt. 5:7, NIV) We bring the shaping influences of our lives into the present, but we need not be defined by them. Through Christ, we are redefined. Christ redeems us; He makes all things new. (Rev. 21:5, NIV)

On the Road to Becoming

Taking this journey with Jesus, moving away from the family gods, being redefined and reshaped by Him, requires faith and vision.

Faith assures us that God makes in us a new creation—we need not be stuck in the past. The hard truth of this is that it is not easy to walk with Him. It means we must let go of the destructive patterns we hold so dear, the old passions and -isms. Though they have given us our sense of self for so many years, they are no longer helpful to us. With faith, we explore the new creation that God is making in us and through us.

Vision allows us to see our freedom in Christ before we ever experience it. The road before us may be long, or dusty, or curvy, yet somehow we have this sense that it is *this* road, no other, that is the kingdom road. It is this kind of vision that inspires the hope that is set before us.

Becoming together

The beautiful truth of the matter is that family and kingdom are one and the same in Christ.

As we "work out [our] own salvation with fear and trembling," (Ph. 2:12) becoming new creations, redefined by Christ, we do not do so in a vacuum. We do it together. We suffer together, we rejoice together, we dream together.

We are travelers on a journey/
fellow pilgrims on the road;
we are here to help each other/
walk the mile and bear the load.

I will hold the Christ-light for you/
in the nighttime of your fear;
I will hold my hand out to you,
Speak the peace you long to hear.

—Gillard, *The Servant Song*

And let me be very clear about this: Jesus put his life on the line right here. This simple teaching on family was also a bold political statement. This is the subtext, and we cannot miss it. "Whoever does the will of God [not Caesar], or whoever hears the *logos* of God [not Caesar] and does it . . ." He was proclaiming here that 'it is not Caiaphas, Pontius Pilate, Herod Antipas or Caesar who holds the reigns of the kingdom, nor is it Father Abraham.' It is not Deval Patrick, John Boehner or Barack Obama who holds God's kingdom together, nor is it pastor or high priest.

Our family, our kingdom, has at its head the King of Kings and Lord of Lords. Government does not justify us; religion does not save us. Only being in community, and fellowship, or what the Greeks called *koinonia*, with Jesus Christ does that.

We are **His** family, **His** kingdom as we move together in **His** grace. This kingdom is not built on land and possessions, what we have gathered, where we've been, and who we were. This kingdom is not about protecting what we have, living in survival mode, or protecting the family gods. It is built on community with the living God and with each other, proactively sharing that community by taking Community to others, going forward until the day we see God coming to dwell with us in the new Jerusalem. The kingdom is not about being stuck in its own past. It honors and celebrates its past as it moves forward. It is very much a kingdom AND a healthy family.

Defined by What Is to Come

Yet, very few of us come from healthy families, and all of us have things in our past we grieve. At the same time, we all have things we celebrate. As we share them, we honor what has been, even what is, and how God has brought us to this point. The old has passed away, the old family gods and rules. Jesus brings us newness of life. God calls us forward as a nation, a royal priesthood, His own possession, whose character is not defined by what has been, but is reshaped by what is to come.

Picture the people who grow with you and move with you, as you grow and move in Christ: *these* are your mother and brothers and sisters. We are a family, we are a kingdom. It is a blessing to enjoy the journey forward together.

This is the kingdom into which we are invited, the kingdom of God. This is the family into which we are invited, the family of God. This is the kingdom family which walks the road with Jesus, and shares the journey with each other. We shed the old gods of our old ways and claim the One True God as our King.

Father, you are the one who calls us to experience a new kind of family. New relationships, new brothers and sisters, elders and children in faith. You are father to us all. And You are more than that—You are our king, the one who calls us to a new kind of kingdom. God, we pray for the courage to step into your kingdom, to become citizens in Your realm, and to invite others into that life too. Help us to move past the trappings of old, the boundaries of former hurts and misunderstandings. Instead, God, let us move into Your kingdom of grace and kindness. Father and King, let us move as Your kingdom people, and as Your precious family.

In Christ, who made family where there was none before. Amen

Study Questions:

1. What are some characteristics of your family that you value?
2. Do you sense certain expectations from your family of origin that make you feel like you are supposed to play a particular role? Is that role inhibiting to you?
3. What are some of the healthy rules that your family lived by? What are some rules that perhaps were not so healthy?
4. Family gods can be just about anything, heroic people, cherished family stories, even treasured objects upon which a high value was placed (a car, a particular chair, even a vase or other heirloom). Describe some of the family gods that had great significance, for good or ill, to your family.
5. Are there issues in your life right now that keep you from freely exercising your faith? Name some of your own personal gods or personal rules that stand in your way. (For instance, worry might be a personal rule or personal god that is difficult to set aside)

6. Who is in your life right now who encourages you to grow or move beyond the limits of the past in spiritually healthy ways?

7. Are there ways that you can be more intentional about connecting with this 'new family'?

8. Are there ways that you can be intentional about exercising your faith for the benefit of yourself <u>and</u> others?

9. Are there new roles that you would like to play in your new family, roles for which you are gifted?

CHAPTER 3

The Sower

I Don't Know What I'm Doing, and I Love It

There are things I operate every day but don't know how they work:

> My computer, a car, running water, an electric can opener, a bike (okay, truthfully I do not operate that every day).

What would happen if you took something apart, deconstructed it so that it no longer worked or had beauty to it?

As a young man, I was fascinated by biology. Naturally, my undergraduate degree in zoology focused on anatomy and physiology. I wasn't sure, though, how I would make a living in that field, so I took a job in a research firm, dropped out of college for a couple of years, and learned how to dissect animals for a living. Trust me when I say that, at the time, there were valid reasons for doing this type of lab research. Within no time, I was up to my elbows in rat and mouse parts. I could get an animal into 100 well-defined pieces in minutes. And I could recognize diseased tissue, describe it thoroughly and keep moving easily through the work all the way to meal-time.

What I could not do was put an animal back together and make it work again. With dissection came death and an end to all the innate beauty God had bestowed in the animal.

Mark 4:26-29

And He was saying, "The kingdom of God is like a man who casts seed upon the soil; and he goes to bed at night and gets up by day, and the seed sprouts and grows—how, he himself does not know. The soil produces crops by itself; first the blade, then the head, then the mature grain in the head. But when the crop permits, he immediately puts in the sickle, because the harvest has come." (NASB)

I am a person who likes to be reassured that when I am doing something, that thing that I am doing is actually going to make a difference. It's a bonus to me when it is a positive difference. But more often than I care to admit, I wait to act when all other options are exhausted.

Yes, I am one of those people who will not stop to get gas until the light is blinking. It is so nice to get back in the car and see that the idiot light has gone off.

I am one of those who doesn't call a plumber when the drip first appears. I wait until the drip becomes a steady flow.

I am one of those who waits to de-frag my hard-drive until none of the programs will open. I love it when the computer tells me I have more free space to load junk into it.

And I am one of those who will reluctantly drag myself into a service station—though they are getting harder to find—long after the GPS has lost a signal and I am on the verge of using the name of Jesus all too freely.

That's how it was when I had finally reached the bottom of my spiritual tank, and dragged my wounded self off to find pastoral counseling: warning lights were flashing before me, dingers were dinging all around me, and I had exhausted every other coping method I had in my bag of tricks. I was in a very uncomfortable place. With events both terrible and great happening all around me, I was miserable.

At the moment I made the decision to pick up the phone to schedule an appointment, it was as if God Himself had said to me, "It is time to be refueled. Oh, and by the way, I am going to rebuild your engine. And since we are having a special moment here, let me take the opportunity to tell you that, going forward, you will be moving in a different direction." And I thought, if the gospel is good news, why does it sound so frightening? But, at that point, the reality was for me that if I did not go with God in that moment, the alternative was deadly—I just could not stay on the same path anymore.

Stephen Crane, in *The Red Badge of Courage*, describes courage as the willingness to act when need overcomes fear. That is where I found myself. What courage I had to step out on faith (in a process with which I had no personal experience) was truly a profound spiritual need overwhelming my fear of the devastating unknown.

I can only imagine that the disciples found themselves in the same tough spot. The freedom they longed for could not be found in the governmental oppression of the Roman Empire. The spiritual peace they sought could not be gained in the unending and impossible legal code established and maintained by the Pharisees. The identity they yearned for—the kind of self-image one has where one thinks "my life really matters"—could not be found in the endless drudgery of the fishing cycle: load the nets, cast off for a long day, throw the nets, pull them in, haul the catch to the market, mend the nets, stow the nets, and go home and go to bed to do it all over again the next day.

It is no wonder that when the charismatic force that was Jesus-in-the-flesh came to them and said, "Follow Me," they screwed up the courage to go with Him.

What Are We Doing Here, Jesus?

Now, after traveling with Him some, seeing the healings, hearing His confounding teachings, they were aware that great things were afoot. But what? "Jesus, precisely what are we doing here? I *was* a fisherman, now I'm . . . what?" The disciples may have been thinking what we might think in this position: "We've come quite a ways with you now, trusting that things *will* work out the way they *should* work out, and so far we're not seeing it. Jesus, you don't want us to be about our old jobs anymore;

exactly what are we in this new thing we're doing? How is this all going to work out? Jesus, I need to know!"

"I need to know *before I take another step with you.*"

We all just need to know.

A Simple Tale

It is into this questioning that Jesus tells this simple tale. It is beautiful the way Mark tells it—and interestingly, he is the only one to mention it. This agrarian parable is so simple that maybe the other gospel writers did not feel compelled to use it. But, for Mark, it conveys a crucial component of what kingdom is about, as we shall see.

One of the poignant attributes of Mark's gospel is that he puts us into the heart of stories by allowing us to visualize the event. For instance, it is only in Mark that we see that when the disciples run panic-stricken to the back of the boat to find Jesus (so he can fix their problem), they find Him comfortable on a cushion. In this retelling of Jesus' parable, Mark is so visually descriptive, we can almost hear the crop growing. (In my mind, always when I read this I hear music from the '60's sitcom, *Green Acres*.)

While the detail brings finesse to the story, the simplicity drives the point home. Put simply,

trust brings promise.

Trust

As we are so painfully aware, trust is a difficult character to develop. We want to know why we should trust, what for, what is the payoff, and other equally diminishing pieces of information. Diminishing, because to trust fully is to step out, in faith, without the answers.

To trust is to set oneself upright on a bike, one foot on a pedal, and push off with the other foot. It is to know truly and deeply that if we just keep our feet moving on the pedals, the bike will remain upright—*even if we do not know what forces hold it up, and cannot describe the math formulas that prove that it is possible to go somewhere without skinning a knee.*

Similarly, this parable describes a man who casts seed on soil, fully expecting that when the time is right, a harvest will come in. The man trusts.

We often want to know what is the next big wave in the ocean of churchiness. We want to know so we can grab our boards and ride the wave to Gloryland. We are apt to do demographic studies, develop paradigms, incorporate church growth initiatives, and develop fool-proof ten-year master plans. It is at that point that we feel confident that we can trust that God is in it, He's got our backs, and will see us through to the goal *we* set.

In our private lives, we want to know who is the latest and greatest Spirit-filled leader. Depending on who we are, that could be a speaker and author or a band. But we want to know because we think they might have something relevant to tell us, something that will make everything clearer to us. And with this new insight, we want to have it all figured out, or at the very least have a better grip on things. If we can just get our brains around it, we can get through it. It is always easier for us to get through problems or struggles if we know exactly what to do. We can work a plan, we can be confident with a plan.

And while all of those approaches have value, and are worthwhile, they do not engender trust. Confidence and boldness maybe, but not trust.

Jesus, as always, was very careful in how he told his story. He was not describing a man who has spent years cataloging his successes and failures. He was not describing someone who compulsively scours spreadsheets looking for ways to maximize production. He was describing a man who rather haphazardly scatters the seed on the ground. He *knows* he will get a crop because he *trusts* he will get a crop. He is not informed by his charts and tables and graphs; he is informed by his faith.

His planning and figuring—his *work*—does not lead to his trust. His trust leads to his work. Deep down inside,

> he trusts,
>> he works,
>>> he participates,

because he knows it will make a difference.

The Quiet Confidence of Not Knowing

Jesus went on to describe the man as one who sticks to his routine. He is quiet, confident and apparently clueless. He goes to bed, he gets up. Day in and day out. Finally, the seed sprouts and grows. "How, he does not know." He does not express a need to know.

We do not always need to know the how of something to be able to experience joy in it. As we watch a fine trumpeter play, we can see that there are things going on with her mouth-muscles, and we can see fingers flying up and down over the valves, yet that information alone does not tell us why we enjoy the beauty of the sound and the thrill of the melody as we do. There is a joy in the simplicity of knowing that the sound is pleasing and evocative within us.

One can imagine this sower getting up in the morning and walking to his field. He may stoop to feel the good earth in his palm. Perhaps he breathes deeply through his nose to smell the fragrance of rich soil. He cannot see what is happening beneath the surface, but in the stillness of his heart, he knows that growth is happening around him and beneath his feet. And after glancing across the field, he turns to walk back to his home.

It is a beautiful thing to look around, breathe deeply and just know that growth is happening all around us and even beneath our own feet. It's the growth that only God can give.

When we are at our worst, we feel compelled to take the God-moments of our lives and wrestle them to the ground, and completely take them apart. We deconstruct and dissect in the interest of understanding. We figure that if we can understand the moment, maybe we can understand God better. Perhaps we even rationalize that if we can fully understand, we can re-create.

Yet to dissect is to kill. We may not kill the moment, though we often do, but we most assuredly kill the trust that led to the God-moment.

When we are at our best, we are privileged to witness the growth all around us. We are encouraged that God is active and on the move. We are eager to see what is happening and to dream of what is to come.

The Promise of Harvest-time

And when we do witness God's growth, we, like this seed-sower, are sure that a rich harvest is coming.

Keeping the parable in its proper context, this story is told at a time when the disciples need, more than anything else, a good dose of reassurance. Having seen Jesus at odds with religious leaders, having seen his family try to take him away, chronically having experienced confusion at the depth of his teaching, the disciples need to be inspired by the vision of what it is they are all about. That is where these kingdom parables come in. That is the value of this short, simple story.

It's as if Jesus is saying, "Do you want to know what My kingdom is about? Do you want to know what you are about *in My kingdom*? Hear this story about a man who trusts, and in his trust, he participates. He doesn't understand it all, he just knows that what he does makes a difference."

Jesus finished by emphasizing the blessing of the harvest. *It will come.* For the disciples, the undercurrent to this metaphor was not a threat as they had so often heard it, but rather promise of completion. Jesus here was reassuring his disciples that all that they are about makes a difference in the kingdom.

Jesus, as always, used a fascinating word here to describe the harvest. He said when the harvest "permits." Sometimes this word, *paradidome*, is understood as betrayed or delivered over to, but in this context it carries with it its full agricultural meaning. The image it carries is that of fruit ready to be picked. When a fruit is not fully ripe, it has to be forcibly pulled off the branch, but when it is ripe, it practically falls into the hands. It is as if it 'wants' to be picked. The fruit 'permits' the picking.

When the kingdom of God is fully alive and active, fully trusting in the King of Kings, the harvest permits the harvesting. It is ready, and it *wants* to be gathered up. There is no great mystery here: all of creation groans, and, in its groaning, yearns to be brought back to the Creator.

Sowing the Seed Now

The truly exciting part of this story is that we are invited to be in it right now. The sower scatters seed long before he knows that broadcasting seed is not usually the best way to bring a strong harvest. We are the kingdom that trusts, that participates, that dreams.

We do not understand how it will come to full fruition. The beauty here is that we do not have to wait until we are all well-schooled in the latest evangelism techniques. We do not have to wait until we understand how the latest demographic changes will affect our ministry plans. We do not have to wait until someone else more eloquent than us can visit that distressed person we know. We do not have to wait to become a top chef to work in a soup kitchen. We do not have to have a perfect plan to participate in the action.

We do not have to analyze.

We do not have to reconstruct or deconstruct.

We do not have to dissect.

All we must do is trust, and participate in the work of God around us. In the kingdom of God, we wake up and go to bed, and each day we go out to breathe in deeply the fragrance of God. We hop on, push off, pedal hard and revel in the joy without thinking twice about it.

Hear the call of God.

Trust it.

Dream of the harvest that is promised.

Revel in the joy that is the kingdom of God!

Our great God, teach us as your kingdom people—to hear you, to trust that what you would speak into our lives would make a difference to us and those around us, to dream the dreams that only you can inspire, and to revel in your goodness.

From now, until we meet you face to face. Amen.

Study Questions

1. What are some things you use everyday without understanding how they work?
2. What are some patterns in your life that you follow, good or bad, without knowing why or how they work (or not work) for you?
3. Are there issues in which you withhold trust from God because you do not understand how He can make good come out of them?
4. Are there issues in your life that lead you to think, "if people knew this about me, they would hate me"? Do you see a connection between how you trust others and how you trust God?
5. What experiences have you had that tend to keep you from trusting deeply?
6. Name one thing you would like to try, but hold off because you do not know how it would turn out.
7. Describe an experience in which you took a chance and acted, not knowing how it would turn out, and marvel at how well it went.

8. Name five things going on in your world in which you can see God moving.
9. Is there a situation in which you feel you can make a difference?
10. Of the promises of God, what excites you the most? What activities of God bring the fullest sense of joy to you?

CHAPTER 4

The Seed

Poetry in Motion

Matthew 13:31-32

He presented another parable to them, saying, "The kingdom of heaven is like a mustard seed, which a man took and sowed in his field; and this is smaller than all other seeds, but when it is full grown, it is larger than the garden plants and becomes a tree, so that THE BIRDS OF THE AIR come and NEST IN ITS BRANCHES." (NASB)

The parable of the mustard seed, as found in Matthew, has been sadly misused throughout the years. It is my interest here to try to deconstruct, demythologize, and re-mystify this short parable. This parable is one of the shortest kingdom analogies, but one of the most powerful. It is loaded with historic kingdom imagery, but for it to be correctly understood, one has to perceive correctly the imagery.

In order to make a comparison, I want us to think of the classic
American poem *Trees*, by Joyce Kilmer.

Trees (1913)

I think that I shall never see
A poem lovely as a tree.

A tree whose hungry mouth is prest
Against the earth's sweet flowing breast;

A tree that looks at God all day,
And lifts her leafy arms to pray;

A tree that may in Summer wear
A nest of robins in her hair;

Upon whose bosom snow has lain;
Who intimately lives with rain.

Poems are made by fools like me,
But only God can make a tree.

Kilmer's imagery here is very simple. He is keenly aware that
there is power and beauty in nature around him, far exceeding
anything man can do. And even with all that power, all that
beauty, there is simplicity too. Only God can do that, he says.
We hear words like that and we think, "That's true—gee, isn't
that nice? Way to go God!" Truly, nature is something to be
celebrated.

Yet, that is a simplistic rendering of that poem. Just like in most poems, there are more layers. Were we to delve into those layers, we would find greater meaning.

Context is Everything

One of my least favorite experiences in high school academics was analyzing poetry. I would dread it, and cringe when the teacher assigned yet another poem to study. I thought to myself, "Why do we have to analyze it? Why can't we just enjoy it? And why can't you pick a poem that is either about sports, or one that has a catchy enough meter and rhyme to make it at least half-way fun?" Our task was to pick it apart. The goal was to get at the many layers of each poem. I was pretty bad at it. I did find one technique or trick, however, that made all the difference. If I could figure out why the poet chose that subject, or what stimulated that flow of thought, then I had a shot, maybe, not necessarily of understanding the meat of the poem (that was probably too much to hope at that time) but getting that most coveted 'A' in poetry. In chasing that elusive high grade, I determined one thing for sure: in poetry, the context of thought is crucial to it's meaning.

The same holds true for the parables of Jesus. We have to come to grips with the context of these stories if we are to get the full meaning. Jesus painted word pictures, especially with His parables, and the gospel writers collected them in such a way as to give us the flavor of His teachings. As we grow in our study of Scripture, one of the most important things we can do is to learn how to assimilate the stories and statements about God into one meaningful whole. A fundamental, vital task is to understand what the authors were saying first in their own situation, to the listeners of their day. When we understand that message, then we can apply that meaning to ourselves. Only then can we put together a full, meaningful, vibrant understanding of God and how to relate with Him.

If we leave our understanding of this mustard seed parable at a superficial level, and take it out of its context, we strip it of most of its meaning. For too long the mustard seed has been taken out of the context as we find it in Matthew 13. We have historically bent it, reshaped it, or re-crafted it to support other meaningful messages. As well, we have we have distorted it for our own purposes to support completely unrelated, weak theologies.

The context of this parable is that of a kingdom teaching. In each Gospel where we see a rendering of this parable, it is in the midst of a series of teachings about the Kingdom of Heaven. In pulling it out of that context, we risk reading into it meanings that are not intended. It is helpful to look at how this parable has been misunderstood and misused in order to get a clearer picture of how it was meant to be understood.

Seed Faith: Seed-faith Giving

In one sense, the mustard seed image got co-opted, stolen right out of its original meaning and purpose. The problem is that this parable has been blended with other mustard seed imagery. By doing so, the meaning of this parable, as part of the great kingdom teachings, has been greatly distorted. It has been manipulated. So have we.

The first incorrect interpretation to clear up can be seen as follows. On a family vacation, we spent the night in a motel that had cable television. As we were flipping through one farcical program after another, we paused at a televangelist whose name escapes me. But really, does the name matter? He came out in Armani and gold, teeth gleaming, hair shiny silver, a luster that would be the envy of the throne room of the King. His message was simple, something like this. "I am entrusted by the most Holy of Holies, the Lord God Himself, to do a mighty work in South America. But I cannot do it alone. I need your help. In helping me you are helping God. Trust God. Send me money—it does not have to be much. Maybe all you can send me is a thousand dollars. But that's okay, you just step out on faith here, have faith like a mustard seed, and you send me that money so I can do the work of Almighty God. And see if it doesn't happen. Watch God pour His blessing into your life, ten times, 100 times, a thousand times what you give. Folks, you cannot out-give God, so get on the phone right now. You call now, and watch the blessings of God pour out on you. Call me." And with that, he smiled and winked at the camera! **He was preaching the concept of "seed-faith giving."**

At that point, my boys could not contain themselves, one in hysterics, the other yelling, "Are you serious?!" My wife called out from the other room, "What are you watching?" deeply afraid that she was missing something good, but we could no longer speak in complete sentences for all the laughing we were doing. I could not say honestly that she was missing anything *good*.

"The mustard seed is small, yet becomes mighty. If we will express but a little bit of faith, God will dump blessings on our heads." That seemed to be the message. In what has become known as the Prosperity Gospel, the Kingdom parable of the mustard seed has been trivialized. We are led to believe that God wants us to be happy, healthy and wealthy. If God can take a lowly mustard seed and make it into a huge tree, certainly He will do more for us. Yet, surely, Jesus had more in mind here than a

simple transaction with an unbelievable interest rate!!

Seed-Faith: Faith as a Mustard Seed

Sadly, the mustard seed image now carries with it the baggage of guilt. If you only had faith as a mustard seed,

You could get out of debt
You could break that addiction
You would find the right partner
You would find success.

But because God did not rise to our challenge to Him, we are left with the devastating belief that we are unworthy of His love *because we did not believe hard enough*. We are unlovable and unlovely in God's eyes.

This kind of interpretation is wrong—it is evil and potentially devastating. It starts by taking the image out of context. If you are someone who has struggled because you were taught this idea—if only you demonstrated enough faith then you too would be blessed—perhaps you can come back to some measure of sanity by remembering that this teaching is not about you or me. The truth is we can do nothing to make us worthy of God's blessing. God blesses because it is His nature to bless. God blesses because He is pleased to bless. And God always blesses in such a way as to demonstrate His indescribable glory. The beauty of it all is God knows us so well that He knows how best to bless us.

It is clear that Jesus spent some time emphasizing the teachings about the Kingdom. And since He is calling us to be Kingdom people, what does He want us to understand about this Kingdom He brings to us? This parable isn't about whether or not we have enough faith. It isn't a charming, poetic image about you and I faithfully walking amongst the blossoming trees, with birds chirping, and Thumper thumping, and Doc and Sleepy and Grumpy watching out for us. Unless we ask the question, "How do I fit into that?" this parable isn't even about us. This parable is about God and His Kingdom.

That is not to say that there is only one way to look at mustard seed imagery in the teachings of Jesus. Jesus used it more than once, and in different contexts. To use this parable, however, to support other ideas is to take it away from its original intent. To take this image of a small seed becoming a mighty tree, and use that image to support stepping out on faith in areas like stewardship, relationships or trust is to wash away its true meaning. We can look at this parable that way and garner some truth, but it is only part of the picture. We need to keep this parable in its place, in the body of Kingdom lessons, to get its full power.

Salvation

Another way this parable has been taken out of context is by looking at it as a metaphor for personal salvation. In some ways, it works. In this interpretation, Jesus says, "Consider the mustard seed. See how little it is? And it must be cast into the ground, buried as it were. It must die as it is. But look, it will be reborn into something new, far beyond imagining." This is a lovely image and a good thought. Paul wrote over and over about dying to self so that God's Spirit can be born within us. (2 Cor 4: 11-15; 5: 16-17; Gal 2: 20; Phil 2: 5-9, where Christ is the model; Romans 6: 4) We are new creatures in Christ. This is all very true, and it is tempting to teach this parable in this manner.

But this is a Kingdom parable. Kingdoms are not about individuals. When Jesus spoke this teaching, He was not giving us an image of salvation. He had something else in mind. The parable began, "the *Kingdom of God* is like . . ." As well, had this been a salvation image, Jesus might have used it in His powerful teaching to Nicodemus. "Nicodemus," He might have said, "you must be born again. Look at the example of the mustard seed. It is so small, so fragile. And when it falls to the ground, it is vulnerable. It must die as a seed so that it may be reborn as a mighty tree, where the birds of the air come to nest in its branches." That would have made a lovely teaching, except He did not teach it. With this story, Jesus wants us to know something about the Kingdom of God. (See John 3)

The Church

A third, significant rendering of this parable, though still out of context, may come closer to the truth. It is the idea that Jesus was perhaps speaking of the Big-C Church. In this interpretation, Jesus is the seed, and the mighty tree is the Church. After all, who would have ever guessed that this itinerant rabbi from a small town in Palestine would become the figurehead for such a large religion? But that is what happened. He went to some plain, common fisherman and urged them to drop everything. He gave them a vision of what could be, and they were off to the races, with the generous help, of course, of the Holy Spirit. From one teacher and twelve ordinary guys came the extraordinary religion of Christianity.

Anybody who has to lead a visioning process has got to love this parable. It is filled with promise and hope that things will get bigger. As long as it is bigger and better—bigger programs, better funding—it is going in the right direction. God certainly would not invest in a losing proposition. It is with this train of thought that we encourage people to "join the church—it's God's winning team!"

But even this is somehow off track. It seems to center on the question "What is the kingdom about?" but in practicality it devolves to the answer, "Who cares? Just join it." That demeans the imagery that Jesus chose here. We must come to understand this parable in its correct context, with all of its subtle nuances and with its rich imagery.

An Essential Kingdom Parable

To get to the heart of this parable about the Kingdom, we must think of it apart from other ways it has been used to support related teachings. And we must trust the simplicity of the imagery here as Jesus uses it. It strikes me that Jesus was not an ignorant man. On the surface, that seems obvious. Yet we often, in reading His words, miss important points because we do not look carefully enough at the words He chose. Why would Jesus say that the mustard seed is the smallest of seeds, when it is not? And why would He say it would grow into a mighty tree, when the mustard plant is a tall bush that likes to grow in fields? Clearly, Jesus has something in mind that we do not get with a superficial reading. The deeper truth is below the surface.

The Kingdom of God is like a mustard seed, Jesus said. How did *He* mean that?

The mustard seed, though not the smallest seed, is small nonetheless. It is fragile and vulnerable, and it is quite common. Perhaps that is why Jesus chose it for his example: it was a seed that was very much like His audience, fragile, vulnerable, common. One can imagine Jesus holding out to them a handful of seeds, saying, "Look at these. The Kingdom of Heaven is like these." As they scratch their heads, wondering of His meaning, He then inspires them with images of great hope.

**Images often speak to the soul in
ways plainer speech cannot.**

The Heart of the Tree
By Henry Cuyler Bunner

What does he plant who plants a tree?
He plants a friend of sun and sky;
He plants the flag of breezes free;
The shaft of beauty, towering high;
He plants a home to heaven anigh
For song and mother-croon of bird
In hushed and happy twilight heard-
The treble of heaven's harmony-
These things he plants who plants a tree.

What does he plant who plants a tree?
He plants cool shade and tender rain,
And seed and bud of days to be,
And years that fade and flush again;
He plants the glory of the plain;
He plants the forest's heritage;
The harvest of a coming age;
The joy that unborn eyes shall see-
These things he plants who plants a tree.

What does he plant who plants a tree?
He plants, in sap and leaf and wood,
In love of home and loyalty
And far-cast thought of civic good-
His blessings on the neighborhood
Who in the hollow of His hand
Holds all the growth of all our land-
A nation's growth from sea to sea
Stirs in his heart who plants a tree.

Bunner's poem takes visual imagery and connects it to a meaning beyond the simplicity of the text. There is nationalism here. What Bunner has done is to take something as simple as tree planting and brought into it the concept that all that a tree is and represents, the heart of the tree, is all that is right and good for our nation, from sea to shining sea. Trees show us God's blessings.

Jesus utilized the same craft to build His parable. The specific imagery He used calls to mind two very significant stories from the Old Testament, His nation's history.

A Mystical, Shady Spot . . .

The first is the story of Nebuchadnezzar, in the fourth chapter of the book of Daniel.

Daniel 4:10-12

Now these were the visions in my mind as I lay on my bed: I was looking, and behold, there was a tree in the midst of the earth and its height was great. 'The tree grew large and became strong And its height reached to the sky, And it was visible to the end of the whole earth. 'Its foliage was beautiful and its fruit abundant, And in it was food for all. The beasts of the field found shade under it, And the birds of the sky dwelt in its branches, And all living creatures fed themselves from it. (NASB)

We find out that the tree was Nebuchadnezzar, and he was too big for his own breeches, so God would strike him down. Nebuchadnezzar was a Babylonian king—he held the lives of God's people in his hands. This was unacceptable to God that the Babylonian king would hold His people slaves. God made some changes in Nebuchadnezzar's life. These changes were preceded by the powerful dream imagery we read in Daniel.

Along the same lines, in Ezekiel 31, *Pharaoh* king of Egypt is described allegorically as a mighty tree, greater than all the trees in the Garden. And because of its pride, it was cast down. The prophet spoke to *Pharaoh*, first with soft, flattering words, then finished with rock-hard truth. *"Pharaoh*, you will be cast down."

The imagery of these passages is exactly the same. The meaning is the same: the great promises of earthly kingdoms *never* come to fulfillment.

In Jonah, we see a reluctant witness who heard the call of God and knew what it meant. And he thought "If I do this, God will save all my enemies, will impart His love and grace to them, and I hate them so I am not gonna do it!" So after he did the job he should have done in the first place, he said to no one in particular, "See! I told you." In his bitterness, he went to a hilltop where he got burning hot. We know what happened: God raised up a plant where Jonah could get relief. Adding fuel to his bitterness, relief did not last. The plant died.

In all of these stories, shade is a powerful motivator. Shade is the one place we want to be when we are in the middle of the desert. In all of these stories, shade means relief for suffering. Nebuchadnezzar's tree, *Pharoah's* tree, and Jonah's plant all offer shade. Yet it is shade that does not last. Jesus called the plant and shade imagery to mind, but when He brought it up, He said 'this is a plant *that will not wither.'*

Jesus used hyperbole to drive that point home. He said the mustard seed 'is the smallest of seeds,' which it is not, and it will become not a bush, but a big tree. He added emphasis through exaggeration: *this kingdom will be like no other!*

To be clear, Jesus is not describing an earthly kingdom here, he is conveying to us the Kingdom of the living God.

. . . Where Suffering is Understood

By telling this story, Jesus recalled to them the imagery of both Jonah and Daniel: God interjected himself into both stories by offering aid in the midst of suffering.

Listeners would pick up echoes of Nebuchadnezzar's dream: he was haunted by this image—the oppressor is himself vanquished. God hears our cries, casting down the oppressors, replacing them with the everlasting Kingdom, where whether freeman or slave, truly all the world is shaded, comforted and fed from this tree.

And listeners would have heard in Jesus' words the plight of Jonah. More invested in comfort than in embracing the Kingdom, Jonah *coveted* the message of God so much he refused to *live it out*. Jesus said the Kingdom is about sharing the goodness of God with those who are suffering without Him. In the Kingdom, we are a people who *need* understanding, and we are a people who *offer* understanding. **In this kingdom, we embrace the message of Christ, we carry the message of Christ, and we flesh it out for the sake of others.**

. . . Where Comfort is Shared

Jesus presented an image of beauty, perhaps even serenity: mustard plants don't grow into trees, but Jesus said with this image, "I am making a new kind of kingdom, far exceeding the limitations of what we have experienced from Babylon, or Rome, or even from Jerusalem!"

The Kingdom of God participates as a whole—it is not just your salvation or mine; we are a body that participates in the redemption of the whole world. In the Kingdom of God, we share the cool shade of the tree with all who are vulnerable; we share "the tender rain and the hope of days to be" with all those who are dying for lack of the singular kindness of God in their lives.

. . . Where Restoration Happens

With this parable, we see the mystical, shady spot, where restoration happens.

So . . .

> . . . where there was brokenness, there is mending.

> . . . where there was oppression, there is release of the captives.

> . . . where there was humiliation and hurt, there is humility and forgiveness.

This Kingdom of God is not for heads of state, not for religious potentates, but for the small and feeble: *"Look how small the mustard seed is."* It is for the weak and vulnerable, the birds who need a home: *"Look how big a tree I make for you."* This Kingdom of God is where restoration happens. There are people we know who need to hear that, who need to meet Jesus and sit in the shade with Him. Sometimes we too just need to stop, and sit in the coolness of His shade—to quit struggling to *do* Christianity, like the reluctant witness, and rest in *being with Jesus*.

Jesus invites us: "Rest in My shade."

No matter how oppressive and scorching the sun, God's tree does not wither.

Where are you broken? In the kingdom, you will find mending there.

Where do you find the hardship of oppression? In the kingdom, there you are released.

Where do you experience hurt? In the kingdom, there you will be cleansed.

Come, rest in the shade of Jesus.

Come, enter into the kingdom of heaven.

Father, forgive us that we dream too small. Forgive us that we are so caught up in what is ours that we forget about the needs around us that you task us to handle. We look for tiny patches of shadow to find rest, but you offer huge shady spots where we can be so refreshed that we become refreshing to others. We seek solitude where we can lick our wounds. You offer such healing that it spills over onto everyone around us. Your kingdom is so much grander than we acknowledge. Forgive us our stubbornness, our short-sightedness, and our pettiness. Create in us a bigger picture—your picture. Your kingdom is truly big enough to redeem the world. We want to be part of that—lead us into those opportunities.

In Christ we find our rest, and with Him we share it with the world. Amen.

Study Questions:

1. What is your favorite poem? What does it mean to you?
2. Have you had the experience of an idea coming to mind that soon grew bigger and bigger? Describe it.
3. Where is your shady spot? Where do you find comfort and rest?
4. Who do you know that needs to find that mystical shady spot in his or her life where comfort can be found?
5. Are there areas in your life where you are suffering? Where can you find comfort for those things? Is there a trusted other with whom you can share this burden?
6. Who do you know that needs comforting? How can you offer comfort in a safe, healthy way?
7. What does it mean to you to find rest? Is that thought comfortable or uncomfortable to you?

CHAPTER 5

Kingdom Treasure

Words, Words, Words

From www.thesaurus.com:

Treasure: hoard, apple of one's eye, cache, nest egg, reserve

Economy: prudence, restraint, parsimony, proficiency, stewardship, management

Roget's Thesaurus

Peter Roget was fascinated by words. He lived in the 1800's, a time when dictionaries and standardized spelling came into prominence. He became a physician, and he was what was called a "natural theologian." But as a boy, his uncle committed suicide before his eyes, which precipitated a life-long struggle with depression. His comfort was words. His solace was words. His safety was in words. He loved the way they sounded, the way they worked to encapsulate ideas, and the worlds those ideas engendered. Words were his treasure. Through the seasons of his life, words came to the foreground and receded into the corners of his mind as a tide rolls in and out. Words would always come back to take his attention—a new word, a new thought, a new connection to make, always a new delight. He loved to chew over his words. He kept lists and lists of them. He was ever compiling more lists. He put them aside to invent things, like the slide rule, but he would come back to them and rearrange them. Inventions require new nomenclature—just think on how many new words were spawned by the invention of the computer—and nomenclature demands new words that have to be sifted and sorted. He put words aside to teach and to study, but he would always come back to them.

Because Roget invented the slide rule, engineering catapulted forward for 125 years until the computer and hand held calculator took its place. Architects, chemists, physicists, ship-builders—they all used his slide rule. As significant as that is, though, that is not how he is remembered. He is remembered for his words, his place of safety, his treasure, his thesaurus. The defining achievement of his life was his thesaurus, his collected and arranged lists of words.

We each have a personal thesaurus—a treasury of words we tend to use. Our words express who we are. For others, they are often the most defining thing about us. We often size up a person by the way he or she presents herself visually. We make snap judgments. We look at them and say to ourselves, "Loosen up and let go a little," or "Business in the front, party in the back," or maybe "He obviously doesn't care what other people think." But then when a person speaks, we get a firmer, stronger impression of who she is by the words she uses, or the tone in his voice, or the aggressiveness of his approach. Starting with words, adding inflection and approach, people present themselves on a deeper level. In that space, with our treasuries of words, we start to engage. It is as we engage that we start to make meaningful, life-changing connections. We find out what is most meaningful to each other, and we express the things about which we are most passionate. We express the treasure of our hearts. It is the nature of treasure that is a fundamental key to understanding a beautiful parable about the Kingdom.

Matthew 13:44

"The kingdom of heaven is like a treasure hidden in the field, which a man found and hid again; and from joy over it he goes and sells all he has and buys that field." (NASB)

Known By Our Treasures

Just as we are understood and often defined in the minds of others by the words we choose, we are defined by our personal treasures. It is all too easy for us to look at a woman who owns twenty-three cats (or is owned by them), and call her the "Cat Lady." In my community, I am known as "Flute Guy." When I walk into the post office, the counter guys call back to the sorters, "Watch out, Flute Guy is here." Then I either pick up my packages or I drop off a bunch. They just know I am a lot of work. To them, Flute Guy is high maintenance. Flute Guy is all about receiving instruments, fixing them and shipping them back out. To them, on a very basic level, I am all about flutes:

> it's my identity
>> it's my income
>>> it's my personal economy

and therefore my treasure.

Fortunately for me, I look at flute-making as Paul looked at tent-making (Acts 18:3): it is a means to facilitate that which I am really passionate about. That's what I call my "personal economy." The income I get out of it affords me my spending choices. Beyond that, personal economy is not just about how the cash flows in and out, it is also about who I am in the midst of what I do. Personal economy also expresses my character and ethics. That which I value the most is going to influence the choices I make and the means I choose to get what I want. The treasure of my heart shapes my personal economy. I could be all about flutes and the money I make out of them (indeed, I was at one time), an architect could be all about his drawings and buildings, a software engineer could be totally immersed in the coding he or she does—that's the kind of thing we do when our characters get buried in our work and we become slaves at the altar of busy-ness. If the treasure of the heart is work, or an individual, or a defining moment, or a nice car or boat or house, then the pursuit of it and the having of it skews the trajectory of life. At some point, Jesus tells us, if we want to live as kingdom people, we have to trade in that treasure for another.

God's Treasure . . .

One of the interesting features to this parable is that Jesus used a noun to describe metaphorically the Kingdom of heaven. He used the word *thesauros*, from which we get the word treasure. It is always a noun in the New Testament, never a verb, as in "I treasure you." It is a repository of valuable things, a storehouse, a collection of those things that are precious. It can be both a space, and the things in that space. Matthew gravitated toward this word; he recorded Jesus using it more than any other gospel writer. Perhaps it reflects Matthew's life as a tax-collector.

In this parable, Jesus said there was a treasure hidden in a field. This was no surprise to Jesus' audience. Throughout history in that part of the world, kingdoms came and went; there was an ebb and flow to wealth as well. When a family was part of a realm that was about to die off or be taken, often the family would secretly bury its wealth, and in those instances where the family could not under any circumstance come back to retrieve it, the treasure would remain hidden until time or good fortune would reveal it to another. A similar event happened not too long ago in the British Isles, when a man was out tending his fields. As he looked around, he saw a shiny object in the grass. Upon digging, he unearthed a treasure of tremendous economic and historic significance, a treasure dating back to the Middle Ages and the foundation for the story of Beowulf.

. . . is there a downside?

In Jesus' story, a man is treading through a field that is not his own, perhaps journeying, perhaps picking flowers. We don't know, and to Jesus it did not matter. What matters most here is that when the man sees the treasure, he sees it for what it is. This is not a crisis at his feet. He does not say to himself, "Great, now I have to dig this up. And if I dig it up, I am just going to have to hide it again until I can lay claim to it. Now if I lay claim to it, it's going to cost me and I like things just the way they are. Why did I have to walk through this field today? What a mess . . ." Actually, nobody knows what this guy is thinking to himself, but it is surely not that. Because he knows full and well, at his feet is a God-treasure.

The exciting aspect of this parable is that the man responds in joy. Everything he does from here on is done out of joy. It is his passion to make this the one thing in his life that makes the rest of his life pale in comparison. To secure the treasure he is not driven by fear. He is inspired by a vision. And in that vision, a revelation really, is the absolute assurance that life will be better with the abundance of this new treasure.

Getting to the Heart of It All

Treasures are dear to us, and they are tricky and cruel. They often start as dreams, which become if/then scenarios that play out in our lives.

If I only had this, then I would be able to . . .

If I could only get that next promotion, then I could . . .

If I had the right car, the right bling, the living space that was just so, then . . .

These are the dreams that lead us into traps, visions that lead us on meaningless quests. They are forever steering us toward treasures that have no significance.

Jesus made an interesting comment in his sermon from the mountain as we find it in Matthew 6. In a section where Jesus was hammering on the idea of authenticity, he told his audience this:

> Do not store up for yourselves treasures on earth, where moth and rust destroy, and where thieves break in and steal. But store up for yourselves treasures in heaven, where neither moth nor rust destroy, and where thieves do not break in or steal; for where your treasure is, there will your heart be also. (Mt 6: 19-21, NASB)

For Jesus, treasure and heart were inseparable. We can't love the Jesus-way and treasure another lifestyle more. It doesn't work to suffer through our Sunday morning Christian routines, but live for Friday and Saturday nights. We can't pretend that our faith is that which is most important to us, yet live six days out of the week as if competition with our neighbors, or success in the world, or fun at all costs, is the definition of fulfillment to us. We can't love God and idolize another. As faith, redemption, restoration, healing, goodness and grace become the treasure of our hearts, we find ourselves wanting to live in a whole new field of dreams. And in that space, the ultimate expression of ourselves is found in the Kingdom of God.

Is My Treasure Decay, or Fear, or Both?

In the mind of Jesus, the things we so easily treasure fall into one or two categories. Over the years, my family has kindly given me beautiful sweaters—they know I get cold easily, and I've always been that way. And nothing has been more frustrating than to have a nice sweater for only a season because some annoying moth has come and eaten holes in it. Then like a demon, he goes and gets seven of his little moth buddies and comes back to make Swiss cheese out of it. A sweater like that is useless before it is even worn in.

At the same time, people throughout history have valued the beauty of silver—except silver is a lot of work to maintain. Gold is much easier to keep shiny—it does not tarnish—and therefore has always been more valuable than silver. People don't like it when their shiny things aren't shiny anymore.

Moth and rust signify decay, a loss of permanence and value. A slow, inevitable march . . . Jesus also mentioned thieves, which conveys a quick, victimizing, violating kind of loss.

We cannot help but be afraid when we have been victimized by theft. For some, the fear leads to the desire for retribution.

For others, perhaps it is more the desire just to disappear, to hide. Treasures that draw thieves inspire us to want to hang on to them at any cost, gripping them with white knuckles.

Those precious treasures that we have built up in our minds to be the end-alls and be-alls of our existence are tainted with decay and fear.

The job we have worked so hard for we will protect even if it means stabbing someone in the back.

> The house we desire comes with a mortgage so high we can barely breathe or eat.

> The power ball jackpot we so desperately "need"— and we *know* we will win—certainly justifies buying 500 tickets.

We compromise ourselves in our quest for the treasures we believe will make us complete.

An Economy of Props

We create entire economies around propping ourselves up. Perhaps the thing about homeless people that shocks us the most is that they seem to have no apparent personal economy beyond what they can beg or scavenge. They don't fit in with the rest of us who orient our lives around our precious personal economies, our treasures. I think of the character in

Tolkien's Lord of the Rings, Gollum, whose whole life is tainted by his treasure, "my Precious."

The treasures that prop us up are the
ones that bring us down.

Proverbs tells us, "There is a way that seems right to man, but in the end brings death." (Pr. 14:12) Our personal economics, generated by treasures that are nothing more than false gods, prop us up with shallow dreams and distorted visions.

Perhaps this is the thought that strikes the man in the field so hard: "The personal economy I have worked so hard to build is *nothing* compared to the God-treasure laid at my feet." May we all be hit so hard. If only Jesus would reach into our hearts—like in a creepy B-rate movie—and pull out the baubles and trinkets we treasure and say, "Look at this! Do you see how meaningless this really is?"

Cashing Out to Cash In

The joy of the God-treasure is that we can let go of the hoard we have worked so hard to accumulate. The man in the field shows us the way. He trades in the icons of his life, selling *all* that he has. He doesn't just drop what he had—he ejects it from his life. That which defined him before is no more.

The tent-maker is not just a tent-maker,
the flute guy has a whole different agenda,
the cat-lady has a new purpose in life.

Jesus told us this guy in the field cashed it all in for a God-identity that filled his heart. In joy, not only did he buy the treasure, *he bought the whole field around the treasure.* He demonstrated to us what we all need to come to grips with. To be a Kingdom citizen is to cash out our fragile identities to cash in on something that lasts forever . . . It is to be known by something far surpassing our narrow dreams. It is to express the God-treasure at the center of our souls. It is to be all about it and to be *all about* all about it! This man wants to be all about this treasure, and even about the field around it.

Jesus tells us . . .

. . . our selfish agendas pale in comparison to God's Kingdom quest.

. . . our personal affects are nothing if they do not contribute to the community of God.

The Economy of God

. . . our personal economy is nothing compared to the economy of God.

To become known by the God-treasure, we have to cash out our personal hoards. In joy, we let go of fear and decay, and grab onto the Kingdom of God. For some of us, that might mean replacing the destructive icons of our lives, in exchange for healthier, redemptive images. For others, it might mean repurposing the gifts God has already given to us. Either way, the result is the same: we become *functioning*, *valued*, and *valuable* in the Kingdom of God. Our personal economies are no longer personal—they are given over to the purpose of the covenant community.

> To live as a kingdom citizen is to jettison
> continually the decaying and fear-ridden icons
> of our lives, so we can invest more and more
> in the eternal treasure of God.

This is a treasure that is not measured by the common currency of the world. It is measured by the intangible, priceless currency of the Kingdom: justice, mercy, grace, kindness, the relief of suffering and oppression, love. The currency of the Kingdom, that which shapes our hearts for eternity, is nothing less than the character of God. This is a treasure to rejoice over!

What is your thesaurus? How are you known?

What is your treasure?

What is it that you most fear letting go?

What is it that you see decaying before you that grieves you so?

What is in your life that you hang onto with a white-knuckle, crippling grip?

These are the things Jesus invites us to turn over to him. Replace. Repurpose. Sell off.

Invest in something new.

Take up the treasure that is the kingdom of God.

Father, we admit that we selfishly cling to treasures that really do nothing for us. They are mere idols in our lives. In the silence of the moment, we each confess to a personal horde that we need to get rid of—a secret sin we harbor, an addiction that keeps us from fully participating in Your great work, a desire for stuff we don't need, securities we find in things other than You. We give these to you now. Speak to us, God, and show us the things in our lives that we need to share, to show kindness, to spread goodness, to offer solace to those who are in desperate need of blessing. Show us how to repurpose the blessings of our lives to become blessings to others. You have blessed us so that we can bless—show us now how to do that.

Give us a vision God, for how to use our passions for your glory. Amen.

Study Questions:

1. What words are particular to the kind of work you do that perhaps someone in another field would not know? (what is the jargon of your profession?)
2. Are there words you use frequently to express yourself to friends? Do you find that you use different words

around people you respect but do not know so well? Why do you think we use different word lists for different people?

3. What are three of the distinct memories you have that shape the choices you make with your work, your family or your friends?

4. Name one thing you do every day, that without which, life would take a different shape.

5. Who is the person in your life that gives you most meaning, and why?

6. What is your most treasured possession? Is this something that obstructs your faith, or enables it? Does it need to be replaced or repurposed?

7. What are some ways a person can replace or repurpose the false treasure of his or her life?

CHAPTER 6

The Merchant Who Seeks

A Pearl at Any Price

What is it that you are willing to put your heart into? What do you treasure the most? If you could pick one possession you own that you would take to a desert island—a book, a musical instrument, a photo album, a volleyball named Wilson—what would you take? You are looking at a magazine, and you see something, perhaps an article, a photograph or an ad that so captivates you that you immediately put down the magazine. You float over to the computer and immediately launch a web-search. You start with the basics—Wikipedia, of course, then Google, you might Yahoo or query your Facebook/Myspace community—and your first thousand results you pretty much throw away because that's the silly stuff that everyone else wants. You are after a precious treasure, uncommon, unique. It cannot be found in the first 100 hits, not even hinted at. You get a clue from amidst the barrage of garbage, and it hits you. What you seek cannot be found by sitting at home. You are now on a quest, and you decide that you do not care where that journey takes you. You are off and running. As I am describing this to you, is there some treasure you love that comes to mind? It may be an object, but it also might be a dream that you have harbored for years.

What we all have in common is that we are made with this yearning for seeking a treasure. What is the treasure you seek? What defines your quest?

Matthew 13:45-46

Again, the kingdom of heaven is like a merchant seeking fine pearls, and upon finding one pearl of great value, he went and sold all that he had and bought it. (NASB)

This is not a fancy story. In fact, I believe one of the more beautiful and challenging aspects of this story is that it is so brief. Yet it is so powerful.

There is nothing quite so moving in all of literature as a person on a quest, except perhaps a Hobbit on a quest. Here, we have the image of a merchant seeking, seeking . . . "all his mind is bent on it . . ." as Gandalf would say. It is very easy, though, to be drawn into the image and lose sight of the merchant. A merchant is no one special; he is quite common. A pearl is a thing of beauty. It is quite natural to want to look at the pearl, and believe that is the essence of the parable. Unlike the previous parable in Matthew, where the Kingdom is compared to a treasure, an object of great worth, here the focus is on the action, the seeking of the object. In this parable, the kingdom is not a static object waiting to be found, it is a dynamic force on a journey.

In the story Jesus presents here, a merchant is seeking fine pearls. We would be wise to recognize that Jesus did not say that the kingdom of God *is* a fine pearl, but rather a merchant *seeking after* the finest of pearls.

An Object of Desire

Yet we cannot overlook the tempting beauty and significance of the pearl. What is it about pearls that people find so fascinating?

I began my search (dare I say quest?), knowing next to nothing about pearls, by going online. I searched pearls, pearl history, pearl lore—it is amazing how many different ways there are to search an item. I am proud to say I did not go to Wikipedia. Knowing that the ancients believed that different gems conferred different powers—some for good and some for ill—I was curious to know how pearls were perceived. I started there because I wondered why Jesus made a fine pearl an object of quest, and not, for instance a diamond, onyx or sapphire.

Tears for the Garden

An ancient legend from Ceylon speaks of Adam and Eve who shed tears and created a lake of pearls. The white pearls were believed to be from Eve's tears and the black from Adam's. It was further believed that because man is better able to control his emotions and sheds lesser tears, that explains the rarity of black pearls as compared to white pearls.

It is intriguing to think that ancient Near Eastern cultures would associate the beautifully shaped, translucent object with the first of mankind, the two created by the very hands of God. Those of the Hebrew tradition add another layer onto that:

Hebrew legend claims that pearls were the tears shed by Eve on being banished from Eden.

To seek after the pearl perhaps can be viewed as the quest to be reunited with the Creator God, to return to the innocence of the Garden, to walk once again, blissfully unaware, naked in the presence of God, and be unashamed. In that sense, then the pearl is that great, one-of-a-kind redemptive love that can make restoration happen.

We are a people who long to be restored to our God. As kingdom people, we yearn to be home in the garden of the Lord.

The merchant has found this priceless pearl, which best represents the tears of Eve. As he holds up his treasure to the heavens, the merchant is perhaps pleading, "See, O God, my Lord, I hold in my hand this one great pearl. Eve's tears are my tears now. Bring me home, so that I may never be apart from you again."

A Perfect Love

Perhaps the more world-weary listener in Jesus' audience would have other things on his mind. The society in which Jesus found himself was steeped in the lore of Greek and Roman culture. The lore of a culture is pervasive, even in the lives of those who do not believe it. We readily associate John Kennedy with Camelot, Abraham Lincoln with abolition, and John Wayne with heroism, whether they represented those things or not. The first century Roman world had traditions of its own, and in these, the object at the center of this parable imagery would have another meaning altogether:

Pearls have always been associated with love. The Greeks and Romans believed that wearing pearls promoted marital bliss, and the bond between Psyche and Cupid was often depicted by a strand of pearls. Venus, the goddess of love, was believed to have been born from an oyster in the sea, like a pearl.

Jesus used marriage imagery in many of his teachings. Matthew 25 portrays the Kingdom of God as virgins waiting for the bridegroom. The teaching in John 14, beginning with "In my father's house are many rooms . . . I go and prepare a place for you" is another one of those. Throughout scripture, the relationship of God and his people is compared to a faithful marriage—and at times to a fractured, betrayed marriage. By using the pearl as a symbol, Jesus may have been drawing on this myth that the pearl carried. The merchant seeks the finest of pearls because he is looking for the finest of loves. Upon finding it, he eagerly gives up all that he has.

What would we give to have the finest of loves at the center of our lives? We are inundated by options of how to find "love." And we are so tired of the experience of having our high hopes crushed by the reality of shallow living. Yet we are reminded here that there truly is a pearl of great price, and it is worth beyond all that we own.

We are people who are defined by our search for God's authentic love. As we find it, we shed all of the false 'loves,' shallow experiences that have no lasting meaning. Like the merchant, we invest all that we are in His perfect Love.

Ultimate Justice

Or perhaps the pearl represents justice. A bizarre chapter in the life and mystique of the pearl was the ancient Near Eastern practice of using them to establish justice in criminal cases. The practice was called margaritomancy, a form of divination. Even at the time of Jesus, this practice was not uncommon. Essentially, suspects in a case would be brought before a table, upon which was a pearl under glass. The pearl would be slowly heated as the suspects were interrogated. Pearls will jump due to the expansion from the heat. Whichever suspect was being questioned at the time the pearl jumped was found guilty.

It could be that Jesus was drawing on this imagery. In this case, his listeners would have understood that the merchant came across a pearl whose value was synonymous with true, ultimate and lasting justice. In a culture where casting lots was commonplace, this merchant seeks a truth not based on chance. The perfect pearl will establish perfect justice.

We are a people who seek God's justice. This is not justice based on popularism, nationalism or signs of the times. It is not justice based on chance and whim. We are a people who seek eternal justice

for *all people*,

for *all time*!

A Gift Worth Cherishing

There is another tradition that may play into this as well. Of course, we know, and Jesus knew, that a pearl is a mere trinket, a bauble, the waste-product of an oyster. Back then, though, as now, pearls were highly prized and valuable. His listeners would have been aware of this shocking but revealing story:

[There is] the famous story of Cleopatra, who, striving to rival the [reckless, wasteful spending] of Marc Antony, dissolved in vinegar the pearl of one of her earrings, which had cost $706,800, and swallowed it. (See www.jjkent.com)

It is sad when a relationship goes sour, but this is so bad it is comical. I can only imagine the scene:

"Honey, I have searched the world over to find you a gift that speaks of the essence of my love for you. Please take it."

"Oh yeah, well let me show you what I think of that!"

Pour vinegar. Add pearl. Stir. Gulp.

In modern dollars, $706,800 down the gullet. No one knows for sure if this really happened, but it was a story told of Cleopatra that showed the shocking avarice and waste of those in authority.

When Jesus mentioned the idea of a priceless pearl, his listeners may have been reflecting on the larger-than-life persona that was Cleopatra. She who would come to represent the excesses of the empire could be the vehicle of a great message here, as a lesson in contrast. Cleopatra would take an object of great beauty, dissolve it and drink it. The merchant at the center of this parable focuses his life on finding such a thing, and will ransom all that he has and all that he is to obtain it. This is a Kingdom not based on hedonism, meaningless pleasure, and waste, like the world they lived in. The Kingdom of God values beauty for the joy it conveys. The Kingdom of God seeks it out, and treasures it. Only a fool would trivialize such a thing as this. The merchant would sell all he's got to attain this one pearl.

The Kingdom of God seeks a great pearl. In the context of the larger body of teachings of Jesus, the pearl then takes on its greatest meaning. The pearls left by the first Adam have been replaced by the Pearl of the second Adam (to use the imagery of Romans). There is only one Pearl that can restore us to the experience of the garden. There is only one Pearl that redeems us and roots us in Love. There is only one

Pearl which establishes justice. There is only one Pearl whose beauty is to be cherished. There is only one Pearl that is worth giving all you've got:

The Pearl that is Jesus, the Christ.

Kingdom Activity

It is *that* pearl that the Kingdom is seeking. In this parable, Jesus portrayed a merchant whose entire quest is bent on finding that one thing.

Nowadays, if we are seeking something we use very modern resources. A telephone, even, is way more than what Jesus was picturing when he is describing this merchant. But in those days, a merchant was one who traveled. He often was a walker, and sometimes he would have a pack animal to carry his wares. He collected to make trades, and in the buying and selling of goods, he made a living as he traveled. Sometimes, it was a modest living. It would be enough to send back or take back home some income to support the larger family. Other times, if he was very good at it, he would use his skills at bargaining to great advantage, always selling for more than what he paid, driving a hard bargain and in the process accumulating wealth.

In this story, in just a few quick words, Jesus conveys the idea that this guy is good at what he does. Knowing the value of pearls to be high, his audience would know that if the merchant can afford any pearl, he is a man who knows how to haggle. Through the years, he has haggled a lot. He is a master at the art of it, and does not mind getting in up to his elbows in tough negotiations. Ultimately, he buys, he resells, and he puts some away. Sometimes he takes his savings and diversifies his holdings by purchasing objects as investments. Gold artwork, perfumed oils, a Salvador Dali or Pablo Picasso when one is available—or maybe not. But he is always hunting. He is always aware that what he has does not satisfy his soul-cravings. He is on a life-long hunt for the Pearl.

Jesus said to his listeners that the Kingdom of God is like this man. The Kingdom is seeking, it is questing, it is on the journey of a life-time. At the center of this quest is that great Pearl. But the activity of the Kingdom is all about that Pearl.

There is an undertone, or two, here that should not be missed. There are those in his audience who believe that the Kingdom of God was something that was to come, certainly not in the here and now. To them, Jesus was saying, the Kingdom is seeking *now*.

There were also people who believed that only those who had the right bloodlines or social connections and ethical imperatives were worthy of the Kingdom. 'It would be unthinkable to compare the Kingdom with such people as merchants. Next thing you know, Jesus will be making disciples out of tax-collectors.' Yet nowhere does Jesus state that only those worthy of the pearl will claim it.

The Kingdom is open to any who seek it.

Seeking . . .

The Kingdom of God is a body on the move. We are a people who go with our eyes open. Just as God sheds light in dark places, the kingdom of God goes where it must, each member moving according to his or her gifts. We are a people who know that there is joy and surprise in even the remotest of places, and God can be found there.

So it is that the people of God's Kingdom can find restoration, like the garden, in the oddest of places. Wherever we can find Rest in Him. That kind of rest may be found in a flower garden or a vegetable garden, in the solitude of a mountain or in the frantic pace of an urban soup kitchen.

In seeking the Pearl, the Kingdom embraces a covenant with the great Lover of mankind. No other love can satisfy.

The Kingdom pursues justice. In an unjust world, where individuals are judged not by the content of their character but by the color of their skin, or by which side of an arbitrary border they live on, or by any number of other meaningless attributes, this Kingdom seeks a lasting justice based on the attributes of God.

The poignant feature of this story, not to be missed, is that it does not matter to the story where the pearl is found, only that it is actively sought.

We are a people who seek.

Questing . . .

And we are a people who go with intent to find. We do not move aimlessly, wandering from place to place. A quest has both a hope and an expectation of finding.

Where it seeks rest and restoration, it finds the healing hand of God.

Where it seeks Love, it finds welcome and purpose.

Where it seeks justice, it finds the will to serve without thought of reward.

Where it seeks beauty, it finds Truth.

The Kingdom of God is on the move, and at the heart of it is the Christ of Mankind, Jesus of Nazareth.

Journey of a lifetime . . .

In Jesus, the pearl of great price is found. To be kingdom people is to be present with Jesus in one sense, and yet in a very real way it is to be also always on the move.

> Always seeking new places
> for God to take us.
>
> Always questing for places
> where Jesus longs to be.

In some ways, it is to look for places out in the world, on mission for the sake of the Gospel. In other ways, it is opening the dark caverns of the soul where we have stubbornly refused to let God's grace enter. In either case, the parable of the merchant reveals to us that the journey takes time, perhaps even a lifetime.

To Be Sold Out for the Kingdom

The bold truth in this story is the lengths to which this merchant will go. Sadly, for us, we tend to be people of convenience. If we have to be bothered to step away from the computer, or put down the remote, or, heaven forbid, give someone a couple dollars, then that is a little too much to expect. But Jesus described this merchant by saying he sold *all that he had*. He was willing to drop it all on God.

I cannot imagine what that would look like, if all of God's people were willing to sell all that we have, for the sake of Jesus. We fuss about tithing—really that is sooo Old Testament—and the difficulties of balancing church-life and home-life. But the ethic of the merchant was that his whole being was absorbed in the quest.

The encouragement is this: there *is* a pearl of great price. It is real, it is now, and it is worth everything you and I have got.

The questions we have to think about now are:

How bad do we want Him?

Are we willing to make the journey?

Are we willing to give all we've got for this Pearl?

Lord God, King of the one True Kingdom, make us a people on the move. Help us to continually seek Your ways. Help us to yearn for Your desires. Teach us to love more deeply, teach us to live more justly, teach us to love mercy so much that offering mercy is second-nature to us. Remind us every day to live in an attitude of humility. God these are the pearls we seek. May we never give up the quest for those things which are dearest to Your heart.

In the name of the one who lived the essence of this great calling, Jesus Christ, Amen.

Study Questions:

1. In what ways do you feel you have found what you are looking for? And in what ways do you feel you are still seeking?
2. What does "resting in God" or being back "in the garden" look like to you?
3. How do you see God's love coming at you? *(write a list of experiences you have had in the last 6 months)* How do you actively demonstrate the love of God to others?
4. What are your top three concerns about justice? What are some steps you are taking right now to make a difference in those areas?

5. Do you see yourself as frugal, generous or wasteful? Give an example.
6. In what ways have you grown over the last five years?
7. In what areas of your life do you think you need to grow the most in the next ten years?
8. Are you on a quest? If so, what does it look like? If not, what has you stuck?

CHAPTER 7

The Dynamic Kingdom

Sometimes You Just Feel Like a Bucket of Rocks

My yard has a lot of problems. We have some very nice flower beds, and some spots with rich, green grass, yet in a large part of our yard there is, to put it kindly, fill dirt where there should be rich, nutritious loam. I stand in my yard, and I look back and forth between the flower beds and the fill, and I think how can I make *that* into that. What would it take to make a bucketful of fill-dirt into a bucketful of good, wholesome earth? I asked a gardener that very question. I took a bucket of the rocky, sandy mess in one hand, and a bucket of the flower bed soil in another, and I went to her and asked her, "See this mess in here? How do I get it to look like this other bucket?" She just laughed at me and said. "No way in the world."

In the Gospel of Mark, immediately after Jesus redefines the family of God and by consequence the Kingdom of God, he tells a story. It is his first parable after the appointing of the twelve disciples who would be his closest friends. It is a story about soil. When he finished laying out the parable to his friends, he called this a "mystery of the Kingdom of God."

Mark 4:1-9

He began to teach again by the sea. And such a very large crowd gathered to Him that he got into a boat in the sea and sat down; and the whole crowd was by the sea on the land. And He was teaching them many things in parables and was saying to them in His teaching, "Listen to this! Behold the sower went out to sow; and as he was sowing, some seed fell beside the road, and the birds came and ate it up. Other seed fell on the rocky ground where it did not have much soil; and immediately it sprang up because it had no depth of soil. And after the sun had risen, it was scorched; and because it had no root, it withered away. Other seed fell among the thorns, and the thorns came up and choked it, and it yielded no crop. Other seeds fell into the good soil, and as they grew up and increased, they yielded a crop and produced thirty, sixty and a hundredfold. He who has ears, let him hear." (NASB)

Calling out from the boat, Jesus used very common imagery here for an agrarian society. It is interesting that He would use a farming analogy by the seaside, when a fishing analogy might make more sense to His audience. Perhaps it is for the same reason He spoke in parables in the first place. While the concepts of the kingdom may be simple, we really need to think out what it is we believe, and live it out. As Jesus spoke across the water, surely there were more than a few who were scratching their heads.

Later, when he was alone with his friends, he explained the parable to them. The seed is the word, He said. As the seed is planted in the various types of soil, that word-seed takes root as the soil will allow. The roadside at that time was not like our grassy roadsides. They were hard-trampled, parched surfaces. The rocky ground, a little further away from the road, was less trampled, more broken on the surface, yet still without depth. Still further from the road, there was good soil. It was rich and certainly deep enough, but uncultivated. Thorns and weeds would quickly overtake and choke out the uncultivated word-seed. The fertile ground was well-prepared to receive the seed, far removed from the surface hardened by heedless trampling.

I see myself throughout this story—sometimes I feel rich and fertile for the Word, while at other times I just feel like a hardened trampled roadside.

Impediments to Rooting

There are times when things just do not go as planned:

A young newlywed couple bought a house. Some time after that, to commemorate the birth of their first child, they planted a tree in the front yard. As the boy grew, so did the tree. After about eight years or so, the dad noticed a problem with the tree. It was not bearing any fruit. So the dad mentioned he may just have to cut the tree down. The boy, in fear of losing the tree, carefully mounted some apples in the tree. Later that day, the dad came in the house with a basketful of apples and proclaimed, "It's a miracle! These apples came from that pear tree!"

Not everything goes the way we want it to, not in work, not in church, not in school, not in life. Just because the seed is sown, growth is not guaranteed. Jesus speaks of impediments to vibrant living. It is important to see that in this parable, only one kind of soil bears lasting results.

Impediments to Faith

It is obvious here that three-fourths of the time Jesus describes what is ultimately useless effort. In one scenario, the ground is just too hard, too impenetrable, so that the seed is left vulnerable, unable to become what it was designed to become. The way Luke tells it in his gospel, fleshing it out a little bit, the seed was too close to the road so that it was practically destined to get trampled under foot, and there was simply no chance for that poor seed. Things were slightly better in the second vignette. Here, the word was received with joy, but only fleetingly, as the seed could not take root for all the rocks. It did not take long for the promise of the seed to wither away under the scorching sun. As any good gardener knows, when the rootless plant is overstressed, truly tested, it has no chance. In the third image, the wording as fascinating here in Jesus' own interpretation: when affliction and persecution arise *because of the word,* He said.

Because of the word . . .

We can find an example of this in the letter to the Galatians. They had heard that we are saved by "hearing with faith" (grace), but they fell back on the notion that we are saved by works of the Law. Grace is such an easy concept, yet so very difficult to live out.

Here, in this parable, Jesus acknowledged that sometimes the concepts themselves are too troublesome to live out. There are just too many competing gods—as Jesus called them, competing vines and such. We are so easily choked by our own complexities that we cannot breathe in the simplicity of his love. Every culture battles this, where the objects that come to us as gifts become the objects of our worship, or where the splendor of our intellectual pursuits blind us to the joy of simple truth. *Surely,* we believe, *it must be harder than this.*

And when we fall into that line of thinking, faith suffers.

Impediments to Peace

Likewise, this parable speaks of the trappings that get in the way of peace.

If living as a child of God is about

> peace with Him,
> harmony with Him,
> **covenant** with Him,

then three quarters of the time Jesus here describes futility. Life is hard and leaves us too vulnerable. Life is fleeting, making it too hard to grab hold of anything meaningful. Life is exhausting—a rat race, we have called it—a relentless course of grabbing and getting only to find that all that we have is of no lasting value.

As life becomes the clamoring to hang on or even to get ahead, God's peace is far removed from us.

Impediments to Joy

Jesus said, "I came that you might have life, and have it more abundantly."

Why doesn't it feel that way? We might say, "I gave my life to you, but I haven't always found myself in a bed of roses since then." If the task is to come home, to rest in God, then the real-life experience of the home is often not what we expected or hoped for.

Joy mixed with grief . . .

        peace mixed with strife . . .

                faith with despair . . .

This may more accurately describe how we experience our lives.

I am reminded of my favorite scene from the film *Madagascar*: The penguins have been seeking their true home. When they get there, they find it is not the paradise they expected. As the wind howls across the ice field, we hear one say to his friends, "This sucks." Sometimes coming home means facing hard truths about our lives. For them, home was a frozen, barren wasteland. That may be the time to redefine home as discussed previously (see chapter two). Certainly if the penguins are smart enough to do that, we can too.

The truth here is this: It is hard to sow joy in the barren places—especially when we decide *the barren places will always be barren*.

All-or-None Thinking

This is a great parable for us because it is the one that Jesus interpreted. On top of that, we have interpreted Jesus, and traditionally we have done it this way. We have come to believe that Jesus means there are four kinds of people. The range goes from extremely useful to the Kingdom—influential, gifted we might say—to "don't bother with him, he is hard as stone." We have taken the words of Jesus and used them to justify ourselves and our evangelistic strategies (a term I loathe—people are not the targets of a strategy, we are the desperately needy recipients of grace!).

I am not sure what we are thinking here: "thank God I am the fertile soil." Perhaps. "That girl over there is clearly roadside dirt—glad I'm not that." Maybe. "God chose me. Cool. Too bad about him, though. Oh well, what time is the ballgame on?"

I use these extremes to point out all-or-none thinking. We are either all good, or totally worthless. We have understood this passage for too long to mean there are good people and bad people (or if we prefer, worthwhile people and people not worth the trouble), with a couple of shades in between, though we tend to ignore them. "Don't bother with them, they might ruin what we got." "We need to be targeting folks who, like us, have abilities that would be great to have around the church." "Let's look for diamonds in the rough, so we can polish them up and show them to the world." The good news with this way of thinking is that there are some people you just know are too tough to be saved, so we have come to realize that we need not bother with them. The bad news is **that's wrong.** In this parable, Jesus says the sower sows even in the hard road-side ditches!

The beauty of this parable is not that each one of us is one of these four types of people; the beauty is found in knowing that each of us bears the burden of being all four types of soil. There are parts of each of us where the gifts come pouring out of fertile, rich abundance. Yet, at the same time, in certain aspects of our lives, we may find ourselves in some pretty barren soil. The question is, "What will we do with that?"

It is sad that we rationalize away the hard things we need to look at. Or is it that we pretend that the unpleasant things about us just do not exist? After all, we are the ones who are all good—we are the redeemed. All too often, we trample on our own soil: "I do well on church committees, so its okay that I'm addicted to online porn. It's not hurting anybody." Or we might believe "because I am a good Bible study teacher, it's no big deal that I always spend way more than I earn. That's what life insurance is for."

We operate on the idea that because we are useful in one aspect of our lives, it is okay that we are hardened to other areas of our lives. Yet we might need to know that the very talents that make us productive at work may be the same issues that keep us from being sensitive to the needs of others. In this way, we fragment ourselves, living without the rich integrity God desires for us, deeply rooted in Him.

Turning the Soil

At some point in our faith journeys, we all need to acknowledge that all that *is* is not all that *can be*.

Imagine the possibilities:

I don't have to be stuck in insanity or pain or hurt forever!

We don't have to be a people where everyone looks, talks, acts and thinks the same!

How beautiful it is when I can be the person God made me to be, and you can be the person God made you to be, and in the being together we can create something entirely new!

Turning the soil in our lives means both crisis and opportunity. They do go hand in hand. Turning the soil requires humility, vulnerability, and fearless but not brutal honesty. For a crisis to be an opportunity, however, we have to be willing to let go of what *was*, and by God's grace and power look to what is *becoming*.

Turning the soil means there is Joy in the Garden.

Beauty in difference

Beauty in change

Celebration in growth

Are we willing to be a people who turn over the soil? Or do the hard places have to stay trampled? We tend to invest in the growth that comes easy. We do well with it, and we look good doing it. When we look good, that is good enough. But my experience is the greater gifts are cultivated in the harder soil.

Tilling the Soil

The mystery of the kingdom is in tilling the soil. To do that, we move in God's grace with intentionality. There is purpose, expectation, joy, and life—in places where none of that existed before. The garden in which we live transforms, by God's kindness, from arid to arable. What was impoverished is now rich!

The Kingdom is clicking on all cylinders when it is tilling the soil. Mentoring, accountability, being real with each other, building meaningful community, visioning together, toiling

together, gardening together and teaching others to garden—
all of these are ways we till the soil in the Kingdom of God.

Turning

Tilling

Sowing

Enriching

God's kingdom grows as the life of the Spirit takes root in us. His kingdom spreads as His Spirit is sown in the barren places of the world.

Sometimes You Just Feel Like a Bag of Rocks . . .

The barren places of the world are not just "out there" somewhere. Sometimes they are deep within us, leaving us feeling dead, depressed or withered, like dry bones in the desert. They can be overwhelming, so that sometimes you just feel like a lumpy bag of rocks,

BUT

Jesus says you don't have to stay that way!

The power of Christ is the power to turn even the driest, hardest, most worthless of soils into a beautiful garden,

by God's grace, by God's power, and through His goodness.

In the Kingdom, all the soil is good because He makes it good.

God, you call us to turn the soil, to till the soil.

Help us to give up our trampled places to Your loving, redeeming kindness. Speak Your word into the rocky places. Take root in our depths so that we may take root in Your depths.

God there is joy in your garden, as we fellowship in You. Make that fellowship real, honest and loving,

For Your names' sake. Amen.

Study Questions

1. What is a hard place in your life right now that you need to till the soil so that God's Word can penetrate deeply?
2. Are there areas in your life that you feel that it is useless, since it will never get any better?
3. Describe a part of your life where you have seen the Word take root in what was dry and barren.
4. Is it hard for you sometimes to believe and accept that Jesus forgives even the worst about you?
5. Is it difficult for you to share painful issues because you feel too exposed or vulnerable?
6. Do you function, or live, as though you believe the barren places of your life must always be barren?
7. In what areas of your life have you grown the most over the last ten years?
8. In what areas of your life do you need to grow the most over the next five years?

9. If you were to describe one growth-goal to have accomplished one year from now, what would it be? Is there someone you trust to share that with, who can help you meet your goal?

CHAPTER 8

The Kingdom Feast

Would You Like to Come for Supper?

As I prepared for this teaching, I asked a friend to help me with a visual aid. He has a shaved head, is muscular and has seventeen pieces of ink body art. The Sunday morning that I shared this teaching he showed up in shorts, a 'wife-beater' t-shirt and heavy boots. He was awesome. We got to the church early, and I had him sit on the entryway steps so that everyone would have to pass him. When and if they greeted him, he responded with low guttural responses. Throughout his time on the steps, he maintained an angry look. I hoped he would rattle the cages a bit.

It worked. At the beginning of the teaching, I interviewed him. After thanking him, I turned and interviewed the fellowship.

Questions for Steve:

Did you feel conspicuous, like you stuck out?

At first, yes—I mean, Paul, look at me, c'mon, tank top, tattoos, go figure, y'know what I mean?

How do you feel all dressed up like this?

[He laughed] usually I don't dress like this. Usually I dress a lot nicer.

Did you get the sense that some people were suspicious of you?

Well, some people, yes, but a lot of people walked by and said good morning. So I gave 'em an evil stare.

Jesus says in our story today that you are precisely the person he wants to come to his banquet.

Did you get the sense that you are welcome here, I hope?

At first, no, but when I came into the church and sat down, a lot of people, well, I'd say they were a little skeptical . . . , and I was a little overwhelmed at first.

You should know, we should all know, that *you are welcome here.*

Questions for congregation:

What did you think when you saw him?

Responses included these: "He deserved a hello", "I saw him sit up front and I thought 'he must be interested.'"

Were there any feelings he engendered when you came and saw him?

"I was flattered he wanted to come to our church."

What feelings went through you?

by raising hands they admitted to fear, conflicted feelings of glad and scared, uncomfortable, and joyful (the loudest response)

*We need to understand that we are him. And just like Steve, each of us **is welcome here.** It is exciting to know that we have been invited to this feast by the Master.*

Luke 14:15-24

When one of those who were reclining at the table with Him heard this, he said to Him, "Blessed is everyone who will eat bread in the kingdom of God!" But He said to him, "A man was giving a big dinner, and he invited many; and at the dinner hour he sent his slave to say to those who had been invited, `Come; for everything is ready now.' "But they all alike began to make excuses. The first one said to him, `I have bought a piece of land and I need to go out and look at it; please consider me excused.' "Another one said, `I have bought five yoke of oxen, and I am going to try them out; please consider me excused.' "Another one said, `I have married a wife, and for that reason I cannot come.' "And the slave came back and reported this to his master. Then the head of the household became angry and said to his slave, `Go out at once into the streets and lanes of the city and bring in here the poor and crippled and blind and lame.' "And the slave said, `Master, what you commanded has been done, and still there is room.' "And the master said to the slave, `Go out into the highways and along the hedges, and compel them to come in, so that my house may be filled. `For I tell you, none of those men who were invited shall taste of my dinner.'" (NASB)

Come, Feast with Me

Jesus told the story of a great feast: The master has issued an invitation, and you have accepted. "It's time to come. Won't you come? The Master is expecting you," the servant says. There is a beautiful image here of pomp and circumstance. This is the kind of dinner where, anybody who is anybody would be there. If it's Hollywood, it's Oscar Night. You can imagine the red carpet, and the glitz and glam. If its the CMT Awards, all of the favorite singers are there, in all their denim and sparkles. If it's a fashion show awards, all the supermodels are there, even Zoolander, sporting his classic look, "Blue Steel." If it's high school, it's prom. In Washington, it's election night, and you've been invited to the acceptance party. A select group has been invited. **Everybody who is anybody *should* be there!**

But they are not! That is the surprise of the story. As Jesus told the story, his listeners were taking it all in. A great man has invited those with whom he has a social connection. Not only have they been invited, they have accepted the invitation. So in the part of the story when the servant goes back to collect the guests, the audience expected to hear how the guests arrived to an opulent feast. But that is not what came next. Rather, the guests looked for excuses. "Wait a minute, Jesus, where are you going with this? What are you saying about us?" the audience wondered.

If we care to look, this is what we find out about ourselves: we are easily distracted people—we even have trouble following through on the commitments we have already made. We have all done it. Why is that?

Perhaps we are . . .

> . . . overcommitted.

> . . . tired.

> . . . stuck in a life-pattern that we learned early.

> . . . willing to make commitments just to get someone off our backs.

For whatever reason, we've all gone back on something or another, and it hurt someone. This is what has happened here. The expected guests went back on their commitments to the master.

It is easy to criticize the group and pretend that their reasons are trivial. None of us would ever go back on our word for such meaningless drivel. Jesus, however, did not make this easy. There is great significance in the excuses He presented.

The first reason was land. Having just bought a piece of property, the new owner needed to look at it. This was no small issue: in an agrarian society, subsistence farming keeps a family fed and perhaps might even provide a little extra income. This is vital to both the family and the community. Success or failure rests on the proper use of the land.

Along the same line, the second reason was the investment in five pairs of oxen. Oxen may have been the most expensive farm tool anyone could own, yet the proper use of them can provide a huge payoff for the owner. To get the most out of work animals, one has to understand them, their strengths and weaknesses, their eating and watering needs, and even which individual of each pair should go on each side.

Finally, the audience heard the last reason, a new bride. Surely, we would understand this is no small issue. After all, brides are more expensive than oxen, and more dangerous too if not attended to correctly. And especially in that day and age, when one married a bride, one married a family and household.

On the surface, we see that these are not really trivial, and for a Hebrew listener, the story carried an even deeper significance. These excuses echo Deuteronomy, where there are reasons listed why a man may be excused from battle-service in the Lord's Army. Just as in other conversations Jesus had, He suggests here that these "friends" have used the letter of the law to violate the Spirit of community.

Shackles of Responsibility

The natural response at this point in the story is to ask, "What is wrong with taking care of the blessings that you have been given? Isn't that good stewardship?" Jesus was pointing out how easily "stuff" gets in the way. "There's no time to celebrate, 'cuz I gotta *take care of* my stuff." "There's no time to celebrate, God, cuz I gotta *protect* my stuff."

But it is as we noted previously:

This Kingdom is *not* built on land and possessions, what we have gathered, where we've been and who we were. The Kingdom is *not* about living in protection mode. The Kingdom is built on community with God and with each other, proactively sharing that community by taking community to others, going forward until the day we see God coming to dwell with us in the new Jerusalem. The Kingdom is not about being stuck in its own past. It honors and celebrates its past **as it moves forward.**

In Jesus' story, the master had offered to share his kingdom with those around him. These self-centered excuses left no room for feasting together. Blessings are no longer blessings when they become shackles of responsibility, when they inhibit participation in community. Good stewardship leads to sharing in the kingdom, and to feasting at the table of the master.

A la Carte Living

Too often we feast a la carte—we nibble at life, caught up in our own anxiety, perhaps even afraid to experience the richness of life that God offers. We cling to what has already been given, afraid the kitchen is now empty. When we nibble, we take a little of this and a bit of that, and we never get full.

Our response is "I've got enough," spiritually speaking, though we barely scratch the surface of all that there is before us. We may go to church (however that may be defined at this point in our lives, mega-church, country church or home church), but never really invest in the community of faith. We may pray when we feel in trouble, but never fully invest in a dialog with God. We may believe in Jesus, but never really call Him Master.

And with this attitude we keep God fully at arm's length. We may accept God's invitation but only on our terms.

God In the Hip Pocket

There is a sense that the folks who backed out on the feast were familiar with the host to the point of complacency—or so they thought. They clearly didn't recognize that the master would be *hurt by their actions*.

When relationships become routine, when we take them for granted, when we forget to cherish the ones God has put in our path, we hurt others. We hurt ourselves. The irony is that we become complacent in the very relationships that mean most to us. We get bored. I love my wife, and she loves me. But I know, she gets bored sometimes. Imagine that. To her it's the same old jokes, same old stories. What was a cute, odd way of looking at things, can now be annoying. She can get tired of me. (Those who know us would find that hard to believe, I know.)

As well, those who struggle with addiction know that one of the most powerful myths of addiction is "when I get high, the only person I am hurting is myself." The reality is that when we are in community with others, especially in recovery, then our unhealthy choices hurt those who care about us. And for the Christian who struggles with addiction, the community of faith, the body of Christ, suffers when he or she suffers. If we only reach out for God's grace when the bottom falls out of the bottom, then we are attempting to walk with God in our hip pockets. Like an emergency credit card, we put God in a convenient location where we can reach Him in a moment of crisis.

Jesus points to the people who get complacent with God. "Yeah, great, another banquet. Put me down," we say, but then we're thinking, "I'll have to check my calendar—I sure hope I'm busy." Every now and then we step out of that mode, participate in the festivities, the goings-on, and then it's back to the routine. Occasionally, we get busy doing churchy things when we know we need something only God can provide. This is a faith walk that is both a la carte and God-in-the-pocket: truthfully, it is more like genie-in-the-bottle, where we pull out the stopper when we need God.

There are times, particularly when I am out shopping, that I reach back to my hip pocket. I know that before I left home, I put my wallet back there. Yet it has been hours since the last time I felt it bulging in my pocket. I get desensitized to it being there. **How desensitized have we become when we get used to putting God in our hip pockets, only to pull Him out when we need Him?**

I truly believe that God does not want to be stuck in our hip pockets, to have us become desensitized to His presence. He does not want us to be complacent with Him. The central image of this story is that of a master who yearns to participate in the lives of those around him, to celebrate with those whom he loves. And he longs to feast with those who long to feast with him.

You mean, we're Invited?

Jesus continued his story. His audience was still struggling to keep up. Since the intended guests had not arrived, who would show? As the story progressed, a powerful contrast of the heart became clear.

The master, Jesus said, is angry. "Scour the pavement, beat the bushes!" the master ordered. "Bring on the feast."

Who are these people who came? How did Jesus describe them?

There are two groups described. Verse 21 describes the disenfranchised of the city: the homeless, the ill, the burdens of society. They are not pretty people. They are stinky, smelly people. They are the kind of people we hope would not grace our doorstep. These are people composed of all four soils. They are hardened by the hurts of life, but they are not without their dignity. They are marginalized by us, but not by the Master.

Imagine yourself as one of these people, getting the invite for the first time in your life. It would be, at first, beyond belief. Imagine your hero—think of a name—and then imagine you got an invitation to dinner with that person. I know we're all probably thinking, 'yeah, that'll never happen.' And that's exactly the place you want to be here because that's what they would be thinking, when they get the invitation. And the banquet is now—they do not even go to get a quick shower and a fresh set of clothes. As Jesus tells it, there is an immediacy. In their excitement—"oh my goodness, can you believe it? Let's go!"—they head for the spread!

There's room for more!

Excitedly, the servant comes back.

"We have more room."

The master's banquet hall is bigger than we could imagine. The mustard plant becomes a tree. Five loaves and two fish feed 5000. How often do we think small when God's goodness is so huge? We are perhaps so used to being let down that we cannot dare to dream big. Or perhaps we have been beaten down so completely that we are convinced that 'surely, there is no place for me there.' The good news is, Jesus says,

"There is room, and room to spare."

A feast for Eye-sores

"What shall we do?" the slave asks. Verse 23 shows us the second group, the dispossessed (so homeless, they don't have a town), the foreign, or get this, criminals and their victims, like in the good Samaritan story. The highways and hedges were not the places to find decent folk. That was where you found the perps and their victims. These are the roadside trash, to our sensitive, churchy eyes.

Jesus described these guests in no uncertain terms. They were folks who were unpopular, unloved, unwholesome. They are not what we could call "good sorts of people." **Not only are they ugly and smelly, they are probably even dangerous** . . .

But *they were there*. They responded to the invitation with joy—they recognized they were unworthy to be in the company of the Master. They recognized the great opportunity. And the fact that they were there *made them welcome guests*.

These guests exhibit something that most of us struggle with: they express genuine, heart-felt joy.

How do we do that?

At the best of times, we would like to respond in joy, but it does not come to us naturally. The broken people responded in joy, jumping in spontaneously. We tend to want to think things through, to calculate the costs down the road. In the example Jesus gave, we can learn from those who feasted with the master.

How awkward would it be to show up to a great hall for a formal feast, and not be dressed for the occasion, and not know what fork to use? It did not matter to them. They understood: to invite means to offer to take in whole, to embrace fully; to be invited is to be accepted wholly, to be embraced fully. More than anything, in that moment they wanted to be "a part." When we come to the feast, we need to recognize that, while we are out of place, we are wanted.

We need to **step out of the shadows**, bringing all of ourselves to the master's table: this is what I am right now, and I **so** want to be a part of all this! Like the birds that find safety in the great tree, there is comfort in the Master's banquet hall.

Accept the Master's invitation,

"Come to my feast,"
and, then, truly,
COME TO THE FEAST!

Let's not ignore the invitation anymore, **because** there's food! Jesus, the bread of Life, says, "There's plenty to eat." Imagine the blessing that is to the starving person. The hungry man does not look at the food before him and say, "yeah, that's nice," only to turn away. The hungry woman does not hold the blessing at arm's length. The poor, the crippled, the blind, the lame, the broken people of the world—these are the ones who excitedly embrace the feast and get there *in whatever way they can get there.* They did not jump in their cars, or order up a limo. They did not hop a camel. They came as fast as they could come, limping, tapping their canes, crawling, sneaking (because old habits die hard). They got there however they could get there.

These are the people who *long* for the kingdom. They *live* in hope of the kingdom. The master yearns for people like these.

The Master calls us to His feast. In complete and joyful celebration, come to the feast, however you can get there.

What is Kingdom Living?

After all that we have looked at, we must ask, what is kingdom living?

Kingdom living is embracing each day as the first day of forever, celebrating the kingdom that is now and the Kingdom that is to come. Kingdom living is helping others to do the same.

Kingdom living is going forward with God and his people, living beyond the past and beyond the trappings of today.

Kingdom living is removing the barriers we have placed in front of ourselves, the barriers that keep us from celebrating the feast.

Kingdom living is being real and honest by bringing all of ourselves, even the ugly stuff, into relationship with God, allowing him to shape us into who He meant us to be. It also means being real and honest with others, so we can grow and move forward together.

Kingdom living means to be at rest with God. At rest with Him, we move with the movement of God. Kingdom living is not moving opposite God, or pushing God along, but excitedly walking in step with Him, through the guidance of the Spirit, *wondering* and *marveling* at the journey.

Kingdom living is to set our feet under the Master's table, to revel in the company of the King. It is to enjoy fully the spread that is put before us. It is to share, along with everyone else who is thrilled to be there, in the great banquet of the Master.

Kingdom living is to know and to live
out, this truth found in 1 Peter 2:

"Once we were no people, now we are God's people."

God paid a king's ransom for us.

Accept the invitation.

Celebrate.

Welcome to the feast.

You have called us to your table O God. May we be wise enough to partake and to celebrate with you. Amen!

Study Questions:

1. Are there certain types, or groups, of people you tend to avoid?
2. If you struggle with following through on commitments, what are some of the reasons for not fulfilling them?
3. What are some of your biggest distractions to investing fully in your faith?
4. Can you give modern-day examples of using the letter of the law to violate the spirit of community?
5. Are there blessings in your life that you fear losing so much that they have become burdens of responsibility?
6. Are there things in your life (secret obsessions, objects or people) you are not willing to give up to have a more vibrant faith-life? Note: it/they might be the very things that have you thinking 'God would never want me to give that up!'
7. In describing your level of faith activity, are you ignoring the invitation to feast, are you nibbling at some a la carte buffet table, or are you feasting with the Master? How would you describe yourself?
8. Are there certain individuals who you hope will never grace the door of your church or home? Are there people you need to welcome to the feast?

CHAPTER 9

Now What?

In the film, *My Fair Lady*, a flower girl named Eliza Doolittle comes to the eminent professor Henry Higgins to learn how to speak "more proper." Her goal is to perhaps one day own a flower shop. He takes her on as a student, or perhaps protégé is a better word, only his goal is much loftier: he is determined to make her fit to be a consort to a king. In a great ball, attended by the prince, she passes the test. No one can tell she ever sold flowers at a street corner. Eliza has been transformed. It is precisely that for which she has desperately yearned. Sadly, when they arrive back at the home of Professor Higgins, he celebrates his success while she collapses in fear. She has finally come to realize that she no longer fits in the world she once knew. She asks Higgins, who cannot grasp her position, "What is to become of me?"

Now What?

"Friend, your sins are forgiven." That is what Jesus said. And that is good news indeed.

Now what?

This is the question that confronts all of us who come to faith in Christ. Just as the Gerasene demoniac in Mark 5 was left with a gnawing sense of unknowing, we are left with that same feeling. We know that what we were is not what we are to be. And we know that the process of becoming is a great metamorphosis.

To understand the glimpses of truth in the kingdom teachings is to peer down the road a ways into a great adventure with God.

In this new kingdom we have entered, the king himself calls us friend and tells us something brand new about us: our sins are forgiven. Whereas before our identities have been forged by brokenness, deception, shame, and hurt, our new identities are something else altogether. We are kingdom citizens, intent on being about the business of the kingdom.

Fundamentally, to be kingdom people, we need to embrace in the deepest depths of our souls that there are no other gods before God. There can only be one king in this kingdom. It is time for us to put away our false gods. They are only props that help us get from day to day. And they don't really help us anyway. With God in the center, we are intent to move beyond any shackles of the past, intent to seek and bring with us his blessing, intent to proclaim all that God is to us—king, lord, and friend.

Essential to being a kingdom citizen is that our relationship with God cannot be an addiction that takes the place of another addiction. Perhaps the best way to understand this is as follows: if our religiosity does not leave room for justice, growth, forgiveness, grace and mercy, extended toward ourselves and others, then it is a mockery of a covenant relationship with Him. As kingdom citizens, we represent a king who is all that, and we ascribe to His ways. We cannot be the same old people we've always been. We no longer fit into the world from which we came.

Like Eliza, and like the demoniac, we are transformed into something new. In the family of God and the kingdom of God, we seek that newness. No longer defined by the past, we are defined (and redefined daily) by what is to come.

This is an amazing thing to think about, that we are not defined by what we have been, but rather by what we are to be. For myself, when I am in a sound spiritual place, I tend to think that I have been developed through my experiences (my 'walk' with him, to use a churchy phrase) to be who I am. In my moments of weakness, I look to the events of my life that have left me broken and in need of fixing. In both cases, I perceive myself based on who I have been.

But for those who respond to God's call to embrace the kingdom, there is an instantaneous change that takes a lifetime to accomplish: the old definitions no longer hold sway, swept aside by the reality of a new way of being. Beginning with a vision of what is to come, fueled by a joy that only comes from being truly known and truly loved, we crawl,

    we limp,

        we run,

            we fly,

sometimes all at once, into a Kingdom whose Lord says, "Welcome to my home—there is much to share and much to do." In that Kingdom, all things are made new, even its citizens. Wide eyed in wonder, we respond, "Show us what is next!" In the Kingdom of God, that which is next defines that which is now.

For Eliza Doolittle, the answers to her questions are vague and pitiful, based on the constraints of a very narrow vision. Yet for the demoniac, the crisis of his life is resolved with a beautiful stroke of love. In his limited view, the best thing he can think to do is follow Jesus around. In his mind, he probably believes he has nothing else to hold him there. But Jesus gives him hope beyond his dreams—He creates for him a purpose: "Go tell your friends and family (his *people*") all that has happened to you." He probably had to let that sink in a moment. As a demoniac, he was dispossessed. "Did He say, I have a 'people?'" And off he goes.

The Kingdom of God buzzes with delight as God Himself delights in his children. God must take great joy in seeing us transformed. Like Eliza, like the demoniac, like you and like me.

As kingdom people, we have to put our lives in the hands of the king. We are assured that God *is* at work in us, both to will and to work for his good pleasure. God desires that our lives be beautiful. That will only happen when we trust in His goodness, and when we trust in His purpose for us is infinitely more precious than any agenda we could dream up. And it will only happen when we fully believe that kingdom living is designed to take us outside of ourselves into the lives of others, in intentionally redemptive ways. In the kingdom, selfishness has no place, and sacrifice is meaningless unless it lifts another toward God.

All of this takes a lot of faith. We may not understand how it all works together, but we trust that whatever we do is going to make a difference. We may perceive that the road ahead is quite long, but we somehow get that 'journey' and 'destination' somehow blend together somewhere along the way. We may even recognize, in all truth and humility, that we are not worthy of the riches offered in the kingdom, but we jump for joy because God deems us worthy anyway. And in faith, we move with the King who calls us to move.

This is a vision that is way beyond the scope of personal needs. If the kingdom of God is about redeeming the world, then the approach we must take is more than "you and me, God." Jesus articulated a grand vision: the kingdom of God is the family of God. The King yearns for all of creation to be reconciled and brought back to Him, so that the family is made whole and complete again. There is much we can do to make that message of joy become a reality.

Some people sadly labor under the ideology of very personal agendas. At the same time, some are stuck in the muck of the past. Others wander without a hope for what is to be. In all of these and more, we have become isolated and disenfranchised from one another, with no unifying identity.

And yet, Jesus came with a powerful message:

In Christ, we are God's people

We are his temple

God dwells in us and walks among us

He is our God, our Lord, our King, our Master

We are His Family

Welcome

to the

Kingdom of God

APPENDIX

Chapter 1

1 Cor 13:12 For now we see in a mirror dimly, but then face to face; for now I know in part, but then I will know fully just as I also have been fully known. (NASB)

Psalm 51:12 Restore to me the joy of Your salvation, and sustain me with a willing spirit. (NASB)

Psalm 139:13-16 For you formed my inward parts; You wove me in my mother's womb. I will give thanks to You, for I am fearfully and wonderfully made; Wonderful are your works, and my soul knows it very well. My frame was not hidden from you, when I was made in secret, and skillfully wrought in the depths of the earth; Your eyes have seen my unformed substance; and in Your book were all written the days that were ordained for me, when as yet there was not one of them. (NASB)

Psalm 8:4 What is man that you are mindful of him, the son of man that you care for him? (NIV)

John 3: 3, 5 Jesus answered and said to him, "Truly, truly, I say to you, unless one is born again he cannot see the kingdom of God . . ." Jesus answered [again], "Truly, truly, I say to you, unless one is born of water and the Spirit he cannot enter into the kingdom of God." (NASB)

John 4: 1-26, starting in 22: You worship what you do not know; we worship what we know, for salvation is from the Jews. But an hour is coming, and now is, when the true worshipers will worship the Father in spirit and truth; for such people the Father seeks to be His worshipers. God is spirit, and those who worship Him must worship in spirit and truth. (NASB)

John 3: 17 For God did not send His Son into the world to judge the world, but that the world might be saved through Him. (NASB)

Chapter 2

See also Matthew 12:46-49, Luke 8:19-21

Matthew 13:53-58 When Jesus had finished these parables, He departed from there. He came to His hometown and began teaching them in their synagogue, so that they were astonished, and said, "Where did this man get this wisdom and these miraculous powers? Is not this the carpenter's son? Is not His mother called Mary, and His brothers, James and Joseph and Simon and Judas? And His sisters, are they not all with us? Where then did this man get all these things?" And they took offense at Him. But Jesus said to them, "A prophet is not without honor except in his hometown and in his own household." And He did not do many miracles there because of their unbelief. (NASB)

1 Peter 2: 9 But you are a chosen race, a royal priesthood, a holy nation, a people for God's own possession, so that you may proclaim the excellencies of Him who has called you out of darkness and into His marvelous light. (NASB)

Genesis 12:2-3 And I will make you a great nation, and I will bless you, and make your name great; and so you shall be a blessing; and I will bless those who bless you, and the one who curses you I will curse. And in you all the families of the earth will be blessed. (NASB)

Matthew 11:28 Come to Me, you who are weary and heavy-laden, and I will give you rest. (NASB)

Revelation 21:5a Behold, I am making all things new. (NASB)

Philippians 2:12 So then, my beloved, just as you have always obeyed, not as in my presence only, but now much more in my absence, work out your salvation with fear and trembling. (NASB)

Richard Gillard, *The Servant Song*, as found in The Baptist Hymnal, copyright 1991, Convention Press, hymn number 613

Chapter 3

Stephen Crane, The Red Badge of Courage, http://www.redbadgeofcourage.org/text.html, see especially chapter 12, where Henry must either move or be swallowed up by the enemy

Mark 4:38-40 Jesus himself was in the stern, asleep on the cushion; and they woke Him and said to Him, "Teacher, do you not care that we are perishing?" And He got up and rebuked the wind and said to the sea, "Hush, be still." And the wind died down and it became perfectly calm. And He said to them, "Why are you afraid? How is it that you have no faith?" (NASB)

Chapter 4

Kilmer, Sgt. Joyce, *Trees*, as found in the anthology, Modern American Poetry, Untermeyer, Louis, ed., http://www1. bartleby.com/104/119.html

Unnamed televangelist, truly it is only because I did not catch his name that I do not have this information. I was laughing too hard to hear it.

Bunner, Henry Cuyler, *The Heart of the Tree*, http://oldpoetry.com/ opoem/34882-Henry-Cuyler-Bunner-The-Heart-Of-The-Tree

Ezekiel 31:5-6, 10-11 'Therefore, its height was loftier than all the trees of the field and its boughs became many and its branches long because of many waters as it spread them out. All the birds of the heavens nested in its boughs, and under its branches all the beasts of the field gave birth, and all great nations lived under its shade . . . Therefore, thus says the Lord God, "Because it is high in its stature and has set its top among the clouds, and its heart is haughty in its loftiness, therefore I will give it into the hand of a despot of the nations . . .'" (NASB)

Jonah 4:5-8 Then Jonah went out from the city and sat east of it. There he made a shelter for himself and sat under it in the shade until he could see what would happen in the city. So the LORD God appointed a plant and it grew up over Jonah to be a shade over his head to deliver him from his discomfort. And Jonah was extremely happy about the plant. But God appointed a worm when dawn came the next day and it attacked the plant and it withered. When the sun came up God appointed a scorching east wind, and the sun beat down on Jonah's head so that he became faint and begged with all his soul to die, saying, "Death is better to me than life." (NASB)

Chapter 5

For a good read about Peter Roget, try *The Man Who Made Lists*, by Joshua Kendall (The Berkley Publishing Group, NY, NY, 2008)

Mt 13:44-45, just as in Hebrews, the author argues the dual nature of the Christ as both high priest and sacrifice, here Matthew demonstrates how for Jesus there was a dual nature of the kingdom: it is both treasure and questing.

Paul's role as a tent-maker is briefly mentioned in Acts 18: 3

The Anglo-Saxon treasure find was announced September 24, 2009. It blew open our understanding of the size and type of treasure hoards that were referenced in stories such as Beowulf. The man who discovered it, Terry Herbert, was not allowed to buy the field nor keep the treasure for himself. http://www.nydailynews.com/2.1353/metal-detector-enthusiast-terry-herbert-unearths-5-5-million-gold-article-1.420080

In the movie version of Lord of the Rings, Andy Serkis very beautifully voices Gollum with a sibilant rasp. It is almost as if Gollum is drooling over the "precioussss" every time he thinks of it.

The Proverbs passage is found in 14:12

Chapter 6

For legends regarding tears in the Garden, this was a valuable resource: http://www.helium.com/items/916876-legends-of-the-pearl

For the pearl/love connection, many websites regarding gems and legends conveyed the same basic message. The following site was a good example: http://www.soul-hunter.com/sailormoon/myth/pearl.php

For information on "justice" established with the use of a pearl, see http://www.themystica.com/mystica/articles/m/margaritomancy.html, or do a websearch on the term margaritomancy

For the story of the pearl and Cleopatra, here was a good source: http://www.jjkent.com/articles/pearl-history-mythology. htm. There were many other good tales that showcase greed and avarice, highlighting the pearl. It seems the pearl has quite a legacy.

Matthew 10:1-4 Jesus summoned His twelve disciples and gave them authority over unclean spirits, to cast them out, and to heal every kind of disease and every kind of sickness. Now the names of the twelve apostles are these: The first, Simon, who is called Peter, and Andrew his brother; and James the son of Zebedee, and John his brother; Philip and Bartholomew; Thomas and **Matthew the tax collector** [emphasis mine]; James the son of Alphaeus, and Thaddaeus; Simon the Zealot, and Judas Iscariot, the one who betrayed Him. (NASB)

King, Martin Luther, Jr. *I Have a Dream*, Text Copyright 1963

Chapter 7

See also Matthew 13:1-23, and Luke 8:4-15

Galatians 3:2 This is the only thing I want to find out from you: did you receive the Spirit by the works of the Law, or by hearing with faith? (NASB)

John 10:10 The thief comes only to steal and kill and destroy; I came that they may have life, and have it abundantly. (NASB)

Darnell and McGrath, *Madagascar*, a DreamWorks Animation film production, 2005

Chapter 8

Stiller, Ben, *Zoolander*, Paramount Pictures, 2001

Deuteronomy 20:2-8 "When you are approaching the battle, the priest shall come near and speak to the people. "He shall say to them, 'Hear, O Israel, you are approaching the battle against your enemies today. Do not be fainthearted. Do not be afraid, or panic, or tremble before them, for the LORD your God is the one who goes with you, to fight for you against your enemies, to save you.' "The officers also shall speak to the people, saying, 'Who is the man that has built a new house and has not dedicated it? Let him depart and return to his house, otherwise he might die in the battle and another man would dedicate it. 'Who is the man that has planted a vineyard and has not begun to use its fruit? Let him depart and return to his house, otherwise he might die in the battle and another man would begin to use its fruit. 'And who is the man that is engaged to a woman and has not married her? Let him depart and return to his house, otherwise he might die in the battle and another man would marry her.' "Then the officers shall speak further to the people and say, 'Who is the man that is afraid and fainthearted? Let him depart and return to his house, so that he might not make his brothers' hearts melt like his heart.' (NASB)

Isaiah 29:13 The Lord says, "These people come near to me with their mouth and honor me with their lips, but their hearts are far from me. Their worship of me is made up only of rules taught by men." (NIV)

See Hosea 11, a passage infused with pathos: God loves Israel, "but the more I called Israel, the further they went from me," (v. 2, NIV). There is so much more God wants for us, yet we turn away.

1 Corinthians 12:14-26 For the body is not one member, but many. If the foot says, "Because I am not a hand, I am not a part of the body," it is not for this reason any the less a part of the body. And if the ear says, "Because I am not an eye, I am not a part of the body," it is not for this reason any the less a part of the body. If the whole body were an eye, where would the hearing be? If the whole were hearing, where would the sense of smell be? But now God has placed the members, each one of them, in the body, just as He desired. If they were all one member, where would the body be? But now there are many members, but one body. And the eye cannot say to the hand, "I have no need of you"; or again the head to the feet, "I have no need of you." On the contrary, it is much truer that the members of the body which seem to be weaker are necessary; and those members of the body which we deem less honorable, on these we bestow more abundant honor, and our less presentable members become much more presentable, whereas our more presentable members have no need of it. But God has so composed the body, giving more abundant honor to that member which lacked, so that there may be no division in the body, but that the

members may have the same care for one another. And if one member suffers, all the members suffer with it; if one member is honored, all the members rejoice with it. (NASB)

Matthew 14:16-21 But Jesus said to them, "They do not need to go away; you give them something to eat!" They said to Him, "We have here only five loaves and two fish." And He said, "Bring them here to Me." Ordering the people to sit down on the grass, He took the five loaves and the two fish, and looking up toward heaven, He blessed the food, and breaking the loaves He gave them to the disciples, and the disciples gave them to the crowds, and they all ate and were satisfied. They picked up what was left over of the broken pieces, twelve full baskets. There were about five thousand men who ate, besides women and children. (NASB)

John 6:35 Jesus said to them, "I am the bread of life; he who comes to me will not hunger, and he who believes in me will never thirst." (NASB)

Chapter 9

Cukor, George, dir. *My Fair Lady*, Warner Brothers Pictures (1964)

Mark 5:1-20 They came to the other side of the sea, into the country of the Gerasenes. When He got out of the boat, immediately a man from the tombs with an unclean spirit met Him, and he had his dwelling among the tombs. And no one was able to bind him anymore, even with a chain;

because he had often been bound with shackles and chains, and the chains had been torn apart by him and the shackles broken in pieces, and no one was strong enough to subdue him. Constantly, night and day, he was screaming among the tombs and in the mountains, and gashing himself with stones. Seeing Jesus from a distance, he ran up and bowed down before Him; and shouting with a loud voice, he said, "What business do we have with each other, Jesus, Son of the Most High God? I implore You by God, do not torment me!" For He had been saying to him, "Come out of the man, you unclean spirit!" And He was asking him, "What is your name?" And he said to Him, "My name is Legion; for we are many." And he began to implore Him earnestly not to send them out of the country. Now there was a large herd of swine feeding nearby on the mountain. The demons implored Him, saying, "Send us into the swine so that we may enter them." Jesus gave them permission. And coming out, the unclean spirits entered the swine; and the herd rushed down the steep bank into the sea, about two thousand of them; and they were drowned in the sea. Their herdsmen ran away and reported it in the city and in the country. And the people came to see what it was that had happened. They came to Jesus and observed the man who had been demon-possessed sitting down, clothed and in his right mind, the very man who had had the "legion "; and they became frightened. Those who had seen it described to them how it had happened to the demon-possessed man, and all about the swine. And they began to implore Him to leave their region. As He was getting into the boat, the man who had been demon-possessed was imploring Him that he might accompany Him. And He did not let him, but He said to him, "Go home to your people and report to them what great things the Lord has done for you, and how He had mercy on you." And he went away and began to proclaim in Decapolis what great things Jesus had done for him; and everyone was amazed. (NASB)

2 Corinthians 6:16 . . . For we are the temple of the living God; just as God said, "I will dwell in them and walk among them; and I will be their God and they will be my people." (NASB)

BIBLIOGRAPHY

Anderson, Betty Ann. "The Oracle: Bssm Encyclopaedia." *The Oracle: Bssm Encyclopaedia.* The Oracle, n.d. Web. 7 Aug. 2009.

Bunner, Henry C. "The Heart Of The Tree by Henry Cuyler Bunner." *The Heart Of The Tree, a Poem by Henry Cuyler Bunner. Poets Love Poem at Allpoetry.* All Poetry, n.d. Web. 22 Aug. 2009.

Crane, Stephen. "Untitled Document." *Untitled Document.* Theredbadgeofcourage.org, n.d. Web. 14 Aug. 2009.

Gillard, Richard, *The Servant Song*, in The Baptist Hymnal. Nashville: Convention Press, 1991 Red Badge of Courage

Hefner, Alan G. "Margaritomancy." *Margaritomancy.* The Mystica, n.d. Web. 07 Aug. 2009.

Kendall, Joshua, The Man Who Made Lists: Love, Death, Madness and the Creation of Roget's Thesaurus. New York: The Berkley Publishing Group, 2008.

Kent, JJ. "History and Mythology of Pearls." *History and Mythology of Pearls.* JJ Kent, Inc., 2004. Web. 7 Aug. 2009.

Kilmer, Joyce. "119. Trees. Joyce Kilmer. Modern American Poetry." *119. Trees. Joyce Kilmer. Modern American Poetry.* Louis Untermeyer, n.d. Web. 22 Aug. 2009.

King, Martin L., Jr. "American Rhetoric: Martin Luther King, Jr.—I Have a Dream." *American Rhetoric: Martin Luther*

King, Jr.—I Have a Dream. Michael E. Eidenmuller, n.d. Web. 05 Aug. 2009.

Madagascar, Dir. Eric Darnell, Tom McGrath, Dreamworks, 2005.

My Fair Lady, Dir. George Cukor, Warner Brothers, 1964.

Peel, Janette. "Legends of the Pearl." *Helium*. Helium, 08 Mar. 2008. Web. 7 Aug. 2008.

Reuters. "Metal-detector Enthusiast Terry Herbert Unearths $5.5 Million in Gold." *NY Daily News*. NY Daily News, 26 Nov. 2009. Web. Mar.-Apr. 2011.

The Lord of the Rings: The Two Towers, Dir. Peter Jackson, New Line Cinema, 2002

Zoolander, Dir. Ben Stiller, Paramount Pictures, 2001.

CPSIA information can be obtained at www.ICGtesting.com
Printed in the USA
BVOW08s0758051113

335427BV00001B/2/P